THE

FALL AWAY

FACTOR

Steve Hickey

ONE SENT
BOOKS

Published by One Sent Books
Sioux Falls, South Dakota, U.S.A.

Cover design by Bobbi Gaukel of Pie In The Sky Studios.
Author photo by Candice Schwab of Candice Ann Photography, Inc.

The Fall Away Factor
by Steve Hickey, 1967-

ISBN 978-06159130-7-0
1. Christian Life | End-Times 2. Biblical Studies | Theology.

Printed in the United States of America

13 14 15 16 / 6 5 4 3 2 1

To Caleb

I love seeing your hunger for God,
your passion for theology and
your ambition for ministry.

Hickeys cross finish lines!

Acknowledgements

I know of no place on the planet where people long for the coming of the Lord more, or are being better prepared to be faithful to the end than the INTERNATIONAL HOUSE OF PRAYER in my hometown of Kansas City. It was Mike Bickle's teaching in the OMEGA COURSE that provoked me to write this book. I wrote and taught this in our church as a follow up to his OMEGA COURSE.

A special thanks to my wife, Kristen, and my assistant, Sheryl Horan, for typing and tweaking this manuscript and to my associate, Dennis White—who embodies loyalty over the long haul—for chasing down a few footnotes and references. I appreciate Carter Nesbitt, Katie Hebbert, Randy Bohlender, and Eugenia Brock for their contribution and skill in editing, proofreading and layout. And once again my friend, Bobbi Gaukel of Pie in the Sky Studios, creatively captures the perfect look and layout for my message series and book covers.

Table of Contents

Preface

However, when the Son of Man comes,
will he find a persistence in faith on the earth?
Luke 18:8 (AMPLIFIED VERSION)

In twenty-five years of pastoral ministry, I have never found a way to avoid the pain of people leaving the church. However, working so that fewer people stray from the fold in the first place has proven to lessen the pain.

Jesus, the Good Shepherd, is certainly far more bereaved than I about the subject of this book—the reality that many will fall away at the end of the age. It doesn't matter who they are or what they have done. God never says about anyone, "*Good, I'm glad they are gone.*" God is all too familiar with rejection, and apostasy is surely a tender topic for our God, who is love. No doubt he takes it personally because he loves people.

In his book, "IT'S NOT BUSINESS, IT'S PERSONAL" Bob Sorge writes:

> *To Jesus, the church is not business. It's personal. Jesus is not merely an astute businessman who has found a promising enterprise on one of his planets.... Rather Jesus is a lovesick Bridegroom who has come to win*

the affections of a Bride... Love isn't business, it's personal.[1]

Granted, bailing on your church is not the same thing as betraying Jesus. Yet, there is a connection and they are related.

Church membership covenants mean very little today. They are great until the first conflict, then people somehow feel released from any and all commitments they have made to a local fellowship. If the Bride struggles to stay faithful to each other in good times, how will she fare when the hour of darkness comes? If Jesus is faithful to his Bride, perhaps we should be too. Though I won't devote a chapter to this point, it needs to be made. One of the great antidotes to apostasy is to stay connected in accountability with others. *"Let us not give up meeting together, as some are in the habit of doing, but let us encourage one another—and all the more as you see the Day approaching"* (Hebrews 10:25 NIV). The entire book of Hebrews is about not shrinking back—it's a call to persevere.

> **One of the great antidotes to apostasy is to stay connected in accountability with others.**

There are a number of reasons people turn from Jesus and fall away from the faith. The focus of this book is what I believe to be the seven big causes. My prayer is that what is written here will be preventative. If what I have spelled out here causes even one person to remain faithful to the end, this book will have served its intended purpose.

The lyrics of a popular song by Justin Rizzo and Misty Edwards capture my frequent prayer... *"I want to be found faithful, I want to be found steady, I want to be found faithful 'til the end."*[2]

---

1   Sorge, Bob. *It's Not Business, It's Personal.* Kansas City: Oasis House, page 3.
2   Justin Rizzo | Misty Edwards, *Found Faithful,* © 2006 Forerunner Worship

I pray you'll stay the course and encourage others to do the same.

Steve Hickey,
September 2013

CHAPTER 1

Don't let your love grow cold

In the summer of 2006, twenty percent of the adult population at our church took a newly released teaching series called THE OMEGA COURSE, which is a DVD study of the end-times.[1] The response far exceeded our expectations. What does it say when so many people made an end-time course a top priority? Having already gone through it in Kansas City, I felt a strong impression that God would use the OMEGA COURSE in an even greater way in our church than he did the ALPHA COURSE.[2]

Our church went through a delightful spiritual refreshing and awakening when we introduced the ALPHA COURSE (a course which seeks to explore the basics of the Christian faith). More than sixty people were healed, many experienced the baptism of the Holy Spirit for the first time and we saw a number of salvations and deliverances. But that summer of 2006, I had the sense that God would use the OMEGA COURSE in even greater ways to more fully align us with him and prepare us for what lies ahead. Frankly, right now very few in the Body of Christ, especially in the United States, are ready for what's ahead. Most have no idea of what's ahead and many who think they know have ideas

---

1   *The Omega Course*, Published by Forerunner Book – International House of Prayer, Kansas City. 2006. Available at http://store.ihopkc.org/store/product/4093/ Omega%3A-Leader%27s-Tool-Kit/
2   *The Alpha Course: A Practical Introduction to the Christian Faith.* London: HTB Publications, 1979. Check out alpha.org.

more rooted in Christian novels than they are rooted in the Word of God.

Recently I listened to an interview where an Egyptian medical doctor[3] discussed the human body's capacity to withstand tribulation. The doctor was obviously a brilliant and devout follower of Christ. He described how every cell in the human body has a threshold and how the limits of that threshold can be gradually lifted to greater levels. People who live in deserts can go without much food or water and endure direct sunlight day after day for entire lifetimes. By contrast, many people in our nation have difficulty with exposure to summer heat and stay close to their air conditioners.

With some exception, the Body of Christ in the West has a very low threshold for tribulation, both physically and spiritually, and the last days will be demanding in every way. Higher gas prices will be the least of our worries as we move closer to the Second Coming of Christ. A key to preparation that is largely missing is the fasted lifestyle that Jesus taught in the Sermon on the Mount.[4] Fasting deepens our commitment and our prayers. It helps our root system in God grow. Our spirituality is soft—our commitments are shallow. Our prayers are soft. Our root system in God has no depth.

I'm borrowing that metaphor from the Parable of the Soils where Jesus said in Matthew 13:21:

---

3 Interview by Kevin Matthews on a CD series called *Cities of Refuge: Prophetic Operations & Strategies for the End-Time Church*. International House of Prayer, Kansas City, 2004. On disk 1 of 4.

4 My conviction is the Sermon on the Mount is THE curriculum churches need to cover in depth over the next few years. At the end of the Sermon, Jesus concluded with a parable of the wise and foolish builders in light of the coming storm. The one who built his life on *"these words"* is the one who prevailed. With that in mind, my recent book on the Sermon on the Mount is the culmination of my long-term fascination with the Sermon and its interpretation. That book is called *Obtainable Expectations: Timely Exposition of Jesus' Sermon on the Mount* and I recommend it to you.

*But since he has no root, he lasts only a short time.
When trouble or persecution comes because of the
word, he quickly falls away.*

Fasting and prayer enable us to go without and lean on God
before we are forced onto the "narrow path."

One of the other reasons believers here in the West have a
very low threshold for tribulation is that we've been taught for
years that the church won't have to go through the Tribulation.
We've been taught that Jesus will Rapture the church before it
gets bad and Christians are always surprised when they discover
there is not one verse in the Bible that supports a Pre-tribulation
Rapture. There are multitudes of verses that talk about the
Rapture; and many more talk about the Tribulation, but there
are none that explicitly put the Rapture before the Tribulation.
What we do have are verses, like in Matthew 24, that clearly
put the Rapture *after* the Tribulation, just preceding the Second
Coming.

Would you be surprised to hear this notion of a Pre-
tribulation Rapture originated in a Plymouth Brethren circle in
Europe in the 1830s? The historic hope of the Church since the
New Testament was written, was always one triumphal Second
Coming. It did not consist of a secretive, elusive Second Coming
for the Church, followed by a "third coming" for all the world
to see. If this surprises you, don't believe me, try to find the Pre-
tribulation Rapture in the Bible yourself—it's not there.

Even the proponents of Pre-trib ideas admit that much—the
late Dr. John Walvoord, from Dallas Theological Seminary
said:

*Admittedly our critics are right; there is no verse that
proves our point. However, we can induce it...*

These are times to get clear about what God's Word is
saying, not build doctrines on inducements - especially if our

> *These are times to get clear about what God's Word is saying, not build doctrines on inducements - especially if our doctrines result in us not readying ourselves properly for what's ahead.*

doctrines result in us not readying ourselves properly for what's ahead. What God's Word says is not always the same as what the television preachers and prophecy shows are saying - I know that it's much easier to listen to Hal Lindsey and Jack Van Impe than it is to look it up yourself. Maybe you aren't listening to anyone on this subject. We cannot ignore this and still obey Jesus - he explicitly commanded us to watch, be vigilant and pray lest we fall asleep and get caught off guard and not have enough oil in our lamps to last the night.

To disregard the end-times is to cut more than one hundred fifty chapters from the Bible.[5] What you will find in the Bible are multiple verses that speak not of a Rapture *from* Tribulation, but of a great falling away *during* it. We need to be far more concerned about falling away than flying away! So far this is all review for those in the OMEGA COURSE, but it's a critical foundation for me to lay before I dive in here to material that is not covered in the course.

> *We need to be far more concerned about falling away than flying away!*

Presented in the OMEGA COURSE are the two extremes related to Jesus' return. Joel 2:11 says: *"For the day of the Lord is great and very terrible; who can endure it?"* It says in Malachi 4:5, *"I will send you Elijah...before... the great and dreadful day of the Lord."* Great and terrible. Great and dreadful. Many are afraid of

---

5   One hundred-fifty chapters of the Bible where at least 51% of the subject matter is related directly to an aspect of the end-times are listed here... http://www.ihopkc.org/resources/files/2011/11/150_Chapters_on_the_End_Times-1.pdf

the end-times but this will be a great time to be alive. Here's a partial listing of positive trends during this time period and you can see there is much to which we can look forward.

+ The greatest outpouring of the Spirit of God is yet ahead

+ The greatest revival ever is yet ahead

+ There will be a great ingathering of souls, miracles

+ The salvation of Israel

+ The Church operating in power and authority

+ Supernatural provision, direction and protection

+ There will be cities of refuge and pockets of mercy

+ The dead in Christ will rise, we who are left will meet Jesus in the air

+ We get new bodies!!

+ Jesus returns to the earth to be king for one thousand years

+ Satan will be bound and thrown into the lake of fire

+ There will be a new heaven and a new earth

There is much to look forward to. It will be a great day! It will simultaneously be a terrible day. There will be…

– An outpouring of the most severe judgments by God ever seen

– There will be great convulsions in nature

– War and rumors of war

– The rage of Satan against the church, retaliation, persecution

– Two severe waves of death where the earth's population is cut in half

- The Antichrist will emerge as the most cruel and evil one to ever live
- A False Prophet will deceive the masses
- There will be an Abomination of Desolation and many martyrs
- And a great falling away, a great apostasy

This book is about this great apostasy.

A good place to begin is with a definition. "Apo" means away and "statis" means standing. The INTERNATIONAL STANDARD BIBLE ENCYCLOPEDIA gives this definition for apostasy—"a standing away from." Those now standing with Christ will step away intentionally for a number of reasons (i.e. offended at God... *"How could a loving God allow..."*). Some will lack spiritual discernment and understanding and fall for a counterfeit peace. Others won't be willing to stand with Israel. The deception factor will be high in those days and some will step away from Jesus, thinking this other fellow has better answers for the world's problems.

Apostasy is the word for falling away from the faith. 1 Timothy 4:1 says, *"The Spirit clearly says that in latter times some will abandon the faith."* 2 Thessalonians 2:3 says, *"Let no one deceive you, for that day cannot come without the coming of the apostasy first, and the appearing of the man of sin"*

Apparently, this falling away will not be a small thing. This verse is telling us it's going to be equally significant of a sign as the emergence of the Antichrist.

It is no secret that membership in mainline churches continues to decline. But this is small potatoes compared to the magnitude of the end-day defection. In 1997, we brought Franklin Graham to our city to do a crusade and thousands came to Christ. Yet I have talked to other pastors in the city about how none of us saw an increase in church attendance. Crusade evangelism is wonderful, but the statistics are not so great. Studies show that only about three percent of those who accept Christ at a crusade end up following Christ. That's a sobering statistic on falling away, but the end-time defection is a defection within the flock. This falling away is not just from the Church; it is a falling away from the faith. It will go beyond backsliding and backpedaling into the realm of betrayal and renouncing core Christian beliefs. There will be many who are now settled in the fold, whose lamp oil will run dry before the night is over. In this book I'm calling for a sobriety of spirit where we wake up to the reality that some who are *for* him today will *not* be for him forever.

There will be those who one day take the "mark of the beast."[6] Many worry if they will accidentally take this mark or if it will be given to them against their will. The answer is *no*. Just like you can't get saved accidentally, you can't take the mark of the beast accidentally. You can't sleep through church, wake up saved because your buddy filled out your card for you.

Salvation is a gift you choose to accept. It will be the same with the mark of the beast. There will be those who get so offended at God that they will consciously decide and commit to *not* stay the course with Christ until the end. Are we sobered up yet?

Having read all the apostasy texts over and over, I comprised a list of seven factors fueling this great falling away.

1. The love of most will grow cold.
2. People will stand on unstable doctrines.
3. Animosity toward Israel will turn many against God's purposes.
4. Horrific events will turn people against God.

---

6 Revelation 13:17

5. Halfhearted devotion will be insufficient to fuel perseverance.

6. As in Noah's day, temporal things will preoccupy many.

7. The cost of discipleship will skyrocket.

In this chapter and those that follow, I'm going to discuss all seven factors fueling this great falling away. Though I have tried to summarize each of them in a short sentence above, they each are assigned an entire chapter in this book because they each are multifaceted even as they overlap each other.

The love of most will grow cold

Matthew 24:12 tells us the great falling away will occur because *"the love of most will grow cold."*

The word *grow* indicates that the cooling off will be gradual. It will take place over time. Love is like a fire that must be fed or it cools off and eventually goes out. Initially, as we first come into God's graces, our hearts are set ablaze and fed by the fact that we are forgiven and set free. Our love for him is fueled by who he is and what he has done. Watchman Nee says, *"By the time the average Christian gets his temperature up to normal, everybody thinks he's got a fever!"*

This is a major factor fueling apostasy. Christians will not be willing to seem fanatical, extreme or judgmental. Some allow the spiritual temperature of the world to cool their hearts. It would be revealing to set a thermometer in your heart. Admittedly, as I consider the state of my heart, there are seasons when multiple fires are vying for fuel. Consider these verses from 2 Timothy 3:1-5 about the *"terrible times in the last days..."*

There will be terrible times in the last days. People will be lovers of themselves, lovers of money, boastful, proud, abusive, disobedient to their parents, ungrateful, without love, unforgiving, slanderous, without self-control, brutal, not lovers of good, treacherous, rash, conceited, lovers of pleasure rather than lovers of God—having a form of godliness but denying its power. In other words, form without fire.

There is much here in these verses but I want us to examine the other flames that are fed in the hearts of those who have the false form of godliness. Their hearts will burn hot after pleasure and wax cold toward God.

In 1 John 2:15-17, we find this passage:

Do not love the world, or the things in the world. If anyone loves the world, the love of the Father is not in him. For all that is in the world, the lust of the flesh and the lust of the eyes and the boastful pride of life, is not from the Father, but is from the world. And the world is passing away, and also its lusts...

James refers to those who love the world as "*adulterers.*" In the last days, many in the church will be found to be in the midst of an ongoing love affair with the world. Every Sunday they convey a false image to others that their marriage to Christ is fine, yet in reality they derive far more excitement from their interaction from the world. The spirit of this world is a cunning seductress who we need to be able to discern and disengage from. Proverbs 7:26 says, "*many are the victims she has cast down and numerous are all her slain.*"

• • • • • • • • • • • • • • • • •

Every Sunday they convey a false image to others that their marriage to Christ is fine, yet in reality they derive far more excitement from their interaction from the world.

• • • • • • • • • • • • • • • • •

Imagine what it would be like on your wedding day to hear your spouse say these words:

> I, Steve, take you, Kristen, to be my lawfully wedded wife. I promise to remain faithful to you on Sundays only—at least two out of four anyway. I refuse to forsake all former lovers, choosing rather to cling to them and pursue them throughout the week...

As ridiculous as that sounds, the Bible says the Church is the Bride of Christ. The love of the Bride will be a key issue in the days to come. It won't be enough to simply sit in church on the weekends.

One of the books on my shelf is called INTOXICATED WITH BABYLON—THE SEDUCTION OF GOD'S PEOPLE IN THE LAST DAYS by Steve Gallagher. Consider what David Ravenhill says in the foreword:

> *The modern-day Church, especially in the West, has its own mistress, having fallen head-over-heels in love with the world. The average believer can talk for hours about "the things of the world," but then try asking about their relationship with the Lord and they quickly run out of words. The Bible says, "out of the abundance of the heart the mouth speaks."*[7]

When a person is in love they will enthusiastically tell you about their beloved. Make no mistake, there is an intense battle for every individual's heart.

Friends, an apostasy is mounting in the Western church. The *born again* are bored with God and are poised to fall first under pressure. Revelation 12:11 says that we overcome by the "*blood of the Lamb and the word of our testimony*." Yet there is more. The verse actually says we overcome, "*by the blood of the Lamb*

---

7   Gallagher, Steve. *Intoxicated with Babylon: The Seduction of God's People in the Last Day.* Dry Ridge, KY: Pure Life Ministries, 1996. Page 9, forward by David Ravenhill.

and by the word of their testimony; and they loved not their lives unto death!"

Those who overcome love one thing. Him. They long for him alone. They are increasingly lovesick for his return. Nothing else about this life has their hearts.

In the very last paragraph of the Bible we read, *"The Spirit and the Bride say, "Come!"*[8] Even so, come Lord Jesus. Notice how in the last days there will be a remarkable unity between the Spirit and the Bride. The two will be in sync. There will be no division between the Spirit and the Church.

Today, there is only a growing unity between the Spirit and the Bride. However many churches, including our own for a season, bring grief to the Spirit and quench the desires of the Spirit's operation in the Church. Some say the Spirit is not really operating in any noticeable way in the Church today. Others teach that the Spirit will be removed from the earth in the last days. Those ideas are nowhere in the Word of God. What we find in the Word of God is such a great outpouring of his Spirit on the Church in the last days[9] that the longings of the Spirit and the longings of the Bride will be the same.

We will see the culmination of the desire of the Spirit and Bride—and what is it? It's an intensified longing for Jesus to come. *The Spirit and the Bride say, Come!... Come, Lord Jesus. You are our hearts desire. Our hearts burn with passion for you.* In the end, God will simply give people what their hearts have desired all along. Those who do not want him in their lives today will not be forced to spend eternity with him. We will all get what we long for. Those with hearts set on temporal things will be greatly disappointed that they were not more lasting.

And those who reject the seduction of the world today won't fall for it later. Don't settle for form without fire. If you want

---

8   Revelation 22:17
9   Joel 2, Acts 2

to foster a hunger for him, start fasting from all the rest. Pray prayers like, *God I want you more than I want my dream house. I want you more than I want anything else. If I don't get you, I'll die and that is okay, too, because you are my promised reward.*

My wife is the one who led the way for me to come out of the realm of form without fire. I used to love a good debate about Jesus being *"the way, the truth and the life"* more than I loved Jesus. Lots of people in the Church are like this. Their faith is about everything but him. We need to come to the place where it's only about him.

I'll give you this passage in two paraphrase translations. It's from the Song of Songs 8:6-7, which is basically about the love between Christ and his Bride:

> *Close your heart to every love but mine; hold no one in your arms but me. Love is as powerful as death; passion is as strong as death itself. It bursts into flame and burns like a raging fire. Water cannot put it out; no flood can drown it. But if anyone tried to buy love with wealth, contempt is all they would get.* (GOOD NEWS BIBLE)

> *Hang my locket around your neck, wear my ring on your finger. Love is invincible facing danger and death. Passion laughs at the terrors of hell. The fire of love stops at nothing—it sweeps everything before it. Flood waters can't drown love, torrents of rain can't put it out. Love can't be bought, love can't be sold—it's not to be found in the marketplace.* (THE MESSAGE)

Pray that passage back to the Lord Jesus multiple times a day this week and watch what happens in your heart. Your desire for him will increase. You will begin to adore him and mediocrity, let alone apostasy, will not be an option for you.

CHAPTER 2

Standing on Unstable Doctrines

In 2005, my wife and I and a team from our church ventured off to Nigeria to spend a couple weeks in the epicenter of a spiritual awakening. Most of the time when American Christians venture off to Africa, they are doing so as missionaries hoping to make a great impact there for Christ. We went for the exact opposite reason. We went to receive impartation and catch on fire with the hopes of bringing that flame back home. Standing in a crowd of millions of people passionately praying and crying out to the Lord is something I will not soon forget. The raw desperation for God to rend the heavens and come down was palpable. Pouring rain did not damper it in the least.

In many ways that trip has been and is being used by God to put us, and keep us, in the fire flow. We saw stuff you don't see here; a mass deliverance, where the minister emerged from an apartment under the enormous platform after twenty-one days of fasting and prayer to simply make a public rebuke before a crowd of millions commanding devils to depart. Everyone stood silent except the demon possessed who started to drop all around us and writhe around on the ground, some like snakes. The ushers carried hundreds of these folks to the mats up front and the minister simply stood over them in silent authoritative prayer until every demon departed and all was still.

How I wished some of my fellow pastors back home were there with me to witness what they have said to me is not real. So many base their beliefs not on the Bible but on what they have or have not personally experienced themselves. If it has happened to them then they will acknowledge its Biblicity. If it has not happened to them, they write it off as for a time long since gone. They are Cessasionists. Cessationism is the first on a list of six unstable doctrines I am convinced are unstable to stand on, especially as we reach the end of the age.

Cessationism versus Continuationalism

Cessationism is the belief that all the supernatural stuff, all the powerful God stuff we see in the Bible, ceased to happen after the death of the last apostle. A Cessationist would say all the gifts of the Spirit, miraculous signs and wonders, deliverance, and healing aren't for today. If weird stuff does happen it's written off as demonic, which is quite ironic to me, as this erroneous doctrine would also say that demons do not have influence today as they did in Biblical times.

There is not one verse that says any of this will end. In fact, Scripture releases this "stuff" to us as tools for our end-time toolbox. All these things not only still happen, but they will happen in greater and greater measure as we reach the end of the age where Satan and the Church have an amazing final clash in which the Church, operating in power and authority, emerges victorious. The opposite of Cessationism is Continualism. Continualism is the belief that God has not removed one gift from the Church. In fact, those in the latter-day Church can expect to do even *"greater things."*[1] If we do not even think there is a devil operating in the world, we will not be equipped to drive him away or discern his deception and we will likely be the first to fall.

---

1   John 14:12

Moralistic, therapeutic deism is what is being dished up in so many churches Sunday after Sunday. It is *deism* in that God does not ever intervene anymore. It is *therapy* as people are only given inspirational feel-goodisms that, at best, help them cope another week. There is no deliverance. It amounts to *moralism*

> **Moralistic, therapeutic deism is what is being dished up in so many churches Sunday after Sunday.**

as what is offered are nice moral things that are good for you whether you follow God or not. God gets mentioned in the generic sense but Jesus is not named except in stories where he is held up as the epitome of a tolerant and caring human being. Make no mistake, the only stable foundation is Jesus and we are well into the days when those who put their full weight on him are deemed extreme. Ironically, they are even deemed unstable while the false foundations of moralistic therapeutic deism are celebrated.

This book is about the factors that fuel falling away. There are multiple passages warning us of a great apostasy at the end of the age. For the sake of review, we have defined the word apostasy as "a standing away from" or a "falling away from the faith." A great tribulation is coming and the Bible says:

> *At that time many will turn away from the faith… many false prophets will appear and deceive many people. Because of the increase of wickedness, the love of most will grow cold.*[2]

In the last chapter, I said the foremost factor fueling the apostasy is that the love of most will grow cold. The idea of falling away stirs up fears in many believers. We wonder how solid and secure we are. Just because you said vows doesn't mean you'll stay married. It's a love relationship we must always keep

---

2   Matthew 24:11-12

in check. So it is with our relationship with Christ. Apostasy is not an option for those who love the Lord. Extinguishing all the other flames in our hearts and stoking the fires of our love Jesus is key. Song of Solomon 8:6-7 bears repeating here:

> *Hang my locket around your neck, wear my ring on your finger. Love is invincible facing danger and death. Passion laughs at the terrors of hell. The fire of love stops at nothing—it sweeps everything before it. Flood waters can't drown love, torrents of rain can't put it out...*

The last chapter was about restoring the First Commandment to the first place. "*Love the Lord your God!*" This brief review is in case you are only reading the chapters of this book that interest you.

Already I have illustrated how a bad doctrine of demons and Cessationism would leave us ill-prepared to ward off darkness and do spiritual work in an effective way. The end-time texts are written to encourage an end-time army of God now assembling to de-throne the "*prince of this age*" at the end of the age. "*Now is the time for the prince of this world to be driven out*" (John 12:31).

1 Timothy 4:1 specifically tells us of increasing demonic activity at the end of the age that fuels the great apostasy:

> ***People will stand on unstable doctrines that will not hold them up and they will fall when all that can be shaken is shaken.***

> *The Spirit clearly says that in the latter times some will abandon the faith and follow deceiving spirits and things taught by demons.*

People will stand on unstable doctrines that will not hold them up and they will fall when all that can be shaken is shaken.

There are specific demonic spirits with specific assignments to infiltrate and corrupt what is being taught in the church. There are demons behind certain doctrines and schools of thought. It seems to me it would be a demon behind these Cessationist ideas that there are no real demons today.

It is like demons are out there in the midst of the path of life swapping out road signs, diverting people with no first hand knowledge of the map. 1 Timothy 4:1 tells us that many will fall away because they have been led away by bad doctrine, doctrines that are propagated by deceiving spirits. We are then warned that these demons and deceiving spirits won't float into Sunday school classes (and the like) and hiss their heresy directly. This next verse says...

> *Such teachings come through hypocritical liars, whose consciences have been seared as with a hot iron.*

Real flesh and blood people will be professing things and propagating ideas that are actually inspirations from hell sent here to trick people into ending up there.

THE MESSAGE paraphrase of this passage says many will abandon the faith and follow the illusions of *"professional liars who've lied so well and for so long that they've lost their capacity for truth."* That's a little softer way of saying it but it is still quite harsh. There is something in me that wants to soften this all up and say something like... *in the last days there will be some teachers who teach things that aren't exactly true.* Did you notice how I left the harsh name-calling out?

But then it dawns on me that Paul softened none of this and that makes me wonder, why? Here's what I have concluded. Paul was hard on this and those who do this because this is a matter of grave concern. Some of the harshest judgments in the Bible are not against sinners, but rather against those who lead others astray—the blind guides—false teachers who set up stumbling blocks which hinder God's children from coming to him.

There is a very important caution given a few verses later here in 1 Timothy 4:16:

Watch your life and doctrine closely. Persevere in them, because if you do, you will save both yourself and your hearers.

Maybe you think you are fine because you are not a teacher. But everyone has a measure of influence over another, parents especially.

Even if what you say is correct, this verse says be sure to *"watch your life"* also because it can mislead in a great way. *Persevere* is a very important word in avoiding apostasy. It means persist, continue, keep at, keep on, stick with and do not give up. The opposite of persevere is to give up and fall away. Apostasy hinges on having and holding onto right doctrine and right thinking about God.

I wrote a book on the Sermon on the Mount underscoring its importance in the end-times as a blueprint for how to live. In Jesus' closing story of the Sermon on Mount, he told the parable of the wise and foolish builder. Maybe you have never thought of this as an "end-time text," but it absolutely is. The inevitable storms that are forecast are not just the inevitable storms of every age. My sense is this parable has its primary fulfillment and culmination at the end of the age when this forecast wave of tribulation is unleashed on the earth. Only those whose "house" or "life" is firmly founded on the Word will last.

Tribulation has a way of knocking people off their life's foundation. It will be the case for those in the Church in latter times whose beliefs are not based on Biblical truth. Numerous passages talk about the latter days being a time of great shaking:

In a little while, I will once more shake the heavens and the earth, the sea and the dry land. I will shake all nations, and the desired of nations will come...[3]

There are many more texts that talk about this coming great shaking and that it will result in a great falling away for those standing on unstable doctrines.

Pre-tribulation Dispensationalism

When tribulation comes we do not want to be standing on unstable doctrines. The first of which, on my list, was Cessationism. Second on my list of unstable doctrines is Pre-tribulation Dispensationalism which is a popular point of view about how the end-times will unfold. The problem with it is there is not one Bible verse that backs up the idea that the Rapture precedes the Tribulation.

Here I will repeat a quote from one of the key Pre-trib proponents who admits his ideas are not exactly taken from the Bible. "*Admittedly our critics are right; there is not one verse that proves our point. However we can induce it...*" I know many love to read the LEFT BEHIND series, but the problem with those books is that it differs from the sequence one gets from the Bible. If you read only the Bible, you will not come to these LEFT BEHIND conclusions.

While we all are chomping at the bit to escape earth, Mormons and Muslims are advancing to take dominion of the earth, which Jesus left us here to do.

While we all are chomping at the bit to escape earth, Mormons and Muslims are advancing to take dominion of the earth, which Jesus left us here to do. He left us behind to do a job and while we are hoping to

---

3   Haggai 2:6-7

31

meet him in the clouds, the Bible says his return puts him right back here on the planet. While we are itching to escape, Jesus is readying to return.

For a long time I thought, *Ah, some people think Jesus is coming back before the Tribulation and others think he's coming back after the Tribulation—the important thing is he's coming back, so let's talk about something else.*

The problem with that idea is it leaves us unprepared for a tribulation. If we think we will not have to go through a time of Great Tribulation, we will not ready ourselves and we will develop no threshold for it. However, if we are leaving right away, we will live detached right now. And there's the problem. This was highlighted during THE OMEGA COURSE:

> *With its doctrine of immanency, (Jesus' return at any moment) some don't emphasize the need for a long-term plan for their lives or ministry—or a commitment to impact society. Why polish the brass on the Titanic? Thus, those with this view usually neglect the cultural mandate of Genesis 1:27.[4]*

While we are busy thinking about going to heaven, the Bible says Jesus is awaiting his return to earth. We need to get all this sorted out and studying the Word of God is the only way to do that.

Passages like Psalm 46:4-5 have end-time significance. This psalm says the earth will give way and nations will be in an uproar. Then we read a line about a remnant of God's people not falling. "*God will help her at break of day.*" The "*break of day*" means the crack of dawn—that moment right at the very end of the night. This verse teaches that the people of God will endure a "night." You prepare differently if you plan to be out all night than if you only plan to be out late into the evening.

---

4 Bickle, Mike. *Omega: End-Time Teaching.* (Kansas City: Forerunner Books, 1996), 89.

The Bible talks about deception being a key factor fueling the end-day apostasy. Deception is already at work in the Church with regard to Christ's return. 2 Peter 3:3-4 talks about the Day of the Lord:

> *First of all, you must understand that in the last days scoffers will come...They will say, "Where is this 'coming' he promised?..."*

In other words, it will not unfold as many thought and people will start to fall away because they thought his coming would be sooner.

Matthew 25 puts this in a parable about the coming of a bridegroom. Ten virgins go out to meet him and he is a long time coming. Five have insufficient oil to survive the night and do not make it to the wedding feast. Many will be lost in the delay. If we took that parable literally, we could say that fifty percent of the Church will not have oil enough to last the night. *God give us oil—fresh oil!*

Once saved always saved?

Third on my list of unstable doctrines is the Doctrine of Eternal Security or *once saved always saved.* Salvation is reduced to saying the sinner's prayer and falling away is never an option. The Doctrine of Eternal Security says everyone who has accepted Christ as Savior will enjoy eternity with God regardless of post-conversion personal conduct. Eternal security is not even logical. We would have to conclude that God will force people to spend eternity with him even though they have turned against him and want nothing to do with him. Somehow a person praying a prayer at summer camp as a kid outweighs a later conscious decision to reject the notion of a loving God who allows bad things to happen.

Related to the Doctrine of Eternal Security is what John Calvin called the Perseverance of the Saints. In Calvinist theology, perseverance of the saints, or the preservation of the saints, refers to the belief that those who are truly elect will remain faithful to the end. Those who fall away were not really ever saved in the first place. That's an easy out but the truth is these passages are not easy. There is great tension here.

There is an age-old debate between falling from grace versus the perseverance of the saints. Many of us grew up under the Doctrine of Eternal Security. We know the passages of Paul that say nothing can separate us from Christ:

> *Shall tribulation, or distress, or persecution, or famine, or nakedness, or peril or sword... No, in all these things we are more than conquerors through him who loved us...*[5]

Jesus said in John 10:28 that *"no one will snatch his sheep from his hand."* So, why then would I list the Doctrine of Eternal Security as an unstable doctrine? The reason is because for every passage like those I have just mentioned there are passages that say:

> *It is impossible for those who have once been enlightened, who have tasted the heavenly gift, who have shared in the Holy Spirit, who have tasted the goodness of the word of God and the powers of the coming age, if they fall away, to be brought back to repentance, because to their loss they are crucifying the Son of God all over again.*[6]

And there are passages that say:

---

5 Romans 8:35-39
6 Hebrews 6:4-6

The one who received the seed that fell on rocky places is the man who hears the word and at once receives it with joy, but since he has no root, he lasts only a short time. When trouble or persecution comes because of the word, he quickly falls away.[7]

There are many more texts like this and there are many more that point to our security in Christ. Considering this interesting tension we have in the Word of God, it would be a grave error to just rest assured on some prayer you prayed in Bible camp as a kid. The Bible says our salvation is something we "*work out.*" It matters how you live right now and whether or not you continue to welcome Christ fully in your life. Philippians 2:12 says, "*Work out your salvation with fear and trembling.*" Saying the sinner's prayer *is vitally* important, but so is the process of our salvation. My intention here is not to imply there is no assurance of salvation. There *is* great assurance and I do believe in eternal security. We are eternally secure in Christ. Those who do not remain in Christ have no assurance of eternal security.

> *Considering this interesting tension we have in the Word of God, it would be a grave error to just rest assured on some prayer you prayed in Bible camp as a kid. The Bible says our salvation is something we "work out."*

We can be assured that as long as we abide in him, all is well. But Jesus said:

If anyone does not remain in me, he is like a branch that is thrown away and withers; such branches are picked up, thrown into the fire and burned.[8]

1 Thessalonians 4:16 is perhaps the most quoted end-time passage in the evangelical church today:

---

7   Matthew 13:20-21
8   John 15:6

> *For the Lord himself will come down from heaven, with a loud command, with the voice of the archangel and with the trumpet call of God, and the dead in Christ will rise first.*

I want to underscore this part—*in Christ*. Staying in him is where our security is found.

Universalism and Syncretism

After false assurances of Eternal Security, Universalism and her sister Syncretism are high up on my list of unstable end-time doctrines. Universalism is the belief that all people will be saved, that God is love and Jesus died for everyone. Therefore salvation is universal and there is then no such thing as eternal punishment. In the last days a "false prophet" will emerge, who is the Antichrist's primary associate.[9] A one-world religion, or a coming together of all the religions of the world, will take place—a syncretism. Syncretism is blending together and assimilating differing or opposite doctrines and practices, resulting in an entirely new religious system in which the tenets of each have been fundamentally changed.

This bumper sticker illustrates syncretism and doctrinal tolerance that is taking root in the earth today.

There is coming a time when Christians who stand firm on Jesus as the only way to heaven will not be tolerated but rather

---

9   Revelation 13, 17-18

fiercely ostracized. Not willing to seem fanatical, many Christians will cave on core beliefs and align with the tolerance crowd.

Recently I checked my IPHONE and noticed a TWITTER status update from Pastor John Piper of BETHLEHEM BAPTIST CHURCH in Minneapolis. Piper's tweet read, *"Farewell Rob Bell."*[10] It included a link to an article where he discussed Pastor Rob Bell's new book, which Piper was calling out as a grand departure from orthodoxy, thus the *"Farewell Rob Bell."* His word "farewell" stood out to me in light of what I have been writing here on apostasy and the falling away at the end of the age.

Rob Bell is an enormously influential, popular and successful pastor in America. Bell's book is called LOVE WINS: HEAVEN, HELL, AND THE FATE OF EVERY PERSON WHO EVER LIVED. The title is enough to convey why this book is presently the topic of conversation and heated controversy. The back cover sows additional seeds of universalism simply by his insertion of three letters and a question mark *"Huh?"*

> *God loves us. God offers us everlasting life by grace, freely, through no merit on our part. Unless you do not respond the right way. Then God will torture you forever. In Hell. Huh?*[11]

A few days after the release of his book, Bell was interviewed on MSNBC by reporter Martin Bashir. An Internet video of the interview was viewed by hundreds of thousands of people in the following week because it was truly remarkable to see even an MSNBC reporter call out his gooey grace. After multiple attempts to redirect his questions and only receiving evasive answers about whether or not he was now promoting universalism,

---

10   http://twitter.com/JohnPiper/status/41590656421863424 February 26, 2011.

11   Bell, Robert H, Jr.. *Love Wins: Heaven, Hell, and the Fate of Every Person Who Ever Lived.* (New York: Harper Collins, 2011), back cover copy.

Bashir finally said to Pastor Bell, "*You are amending the Gospel so that it's palatable.*"[12]

My son Caleb is presently in his second year of an M. Div. program at ASBURY THEOLOGICAL SEMINARY in Kentucky, and he is also a big John Piper fan. Perhaps his interest in Piper stems from our submersion into the world of John Calvin a few summers ago in Geneva, Switzerland. In any case, Caleb is drawn to Piper as an advocate for precise theological thinking. Knowing that, I assumed Caleb would come down hard on Rob Bell's universalism but instead I got a text from him saying he is, "*sad for Bell's kids because he knows how it feels when people berate your dad for what he writes and for the stands he takes.*" Instead of calling down fire on Rob Bell, Caleb was interceding for Pastor Bell's kids.

When I shared this with a pastor friend he said, "*Wow, you can tell he's been with Jesus.*" Another friend said, "*Taking down Universalism is easy; compassion is not!*" Sharing that story with you seems important in this chapter because even as we are faced with gross doctrinal compromise in the days to come, we need to keep our own hearts in check. When Jesus returns we do not want it to be said of us, "*they love to fight about Jesus more than they love Jesus.*"

Gooey grace

The next unstable doctrine on my list of end-time unstable doctrines is cheap grace. Perhaps you are familiar with this term and its origin. The German Christian martyr Dietrich Bonhoeffer wrote about this in his classic book, "THE COST OF DISCIPLESHIP."

> *Cheap grace is the deadly enemy of the Church... Cheap grace means grace sold on the market like cheapjack's wares. The sacraments, the forgiveness of*

---

12   Youtube clip of MSNBC's Martin Bashir's Show – "*MSNBC Host Makes Rob Bell Squirm: "You're Amending The Gospel So That It's Palatable!*" March 15, 2001.

*sin, and the consolations of religion are thrown away
at cut prices...The essence of grace, we suppose, is that
the account has been paid in advance; and, because
it has been paid, everything can be had for nothing...
Cheap grace is the preaching of forgiveness without re-
quiring repentance, baptism without church discipline,
Communion without confession, absolution without
personal confession. Cheap grace is grace without discipleship, grace without the cross, grace without Jesus
Christ...[13]*

Bonhoeffer goes on like this for an entire chapter. Cheap grace is epidemic in Western Christianity. It says, *God loves you just as you are and therefore you need not change anything or live any differently.* The Apostle Paul warned of those who turned grace into a license to sin.[14] Even so, false, yet popular, constructions of eternal security and grace are giving many today a free pass to sin. People then live however they want because God is love and will forgive them.

In the last days, people who today are sitting in churches will fall away because their faith will be resting on religion, yet their hearts will be cold toward Christ. They will cling to their baby baptism, cling to communion, cling to their church membership somewhere and cling to the sinner's prayer they prayed years previously. They will have a memory that they came to Christ, but they will not be willing to follow him and take up their cross.

The False Justice Movement

On Friday evening, July 1, 1981, busy hotel guests walked across a series of suspended walkways, headed to their rooms or out for the evening. In the lobby below, over 1600 people

---

13   Bonhoeffer, Dietrich. *The Cost of Discipleship.* (New York: Collier Books, 1937), 45 and 47.
14   Romans 6:1-2, 15

attended a dance competition. Some were competing, others were simply there to cheer them on. As the evening continued, the crowd size made it difficult to see the participants and many found their way up to the overhead walkways to gain a better view.

Midway through the event, the unthinkable happened. The uppermost walkway separated from its moorings and crashed down on the two walkways below, which in turn fell onto the crowded dance floor.

In what became known as the Kansas City HYATT REGENCY disaster, 114 people lost their lives and many times more were injured. That number was not matched in a structural disaster until the Twin Towers fell on September 11, 2001.

The building had been open for business exactly one year to the day. In that year, it's doubtful that anyone ever used those walkways and questioned their stability. Certainly the night of the disaster, the walkways had the full faith of those standing on them. Regrettably for those involved, it is not our faith in structures or platforms that makes them solid.

The final doctrine I'd like to address is particularly dangerous to young people in our culture. The cry for justice is rising from every corner of our society, yet in many places it is a hollow cry, devoid of the true Giver of Justice. In the foreword to Stuart Greave's excellent book, UNVEILING THE TRUTH ABOUT SOCIAL JUSTICE, Lou Engle writes: *"This emerging generation has been apprehended by a burning call to bring forth justice in the earth, but justice without Jesus can be a global exercise in humanistic paradise building."*

Like those people in the HYATT, they are streaming out onto an unstable platform with no thought that it will come crashing down in time. To make it even more dangerous, it's not a self-serving doctrine that one might suspect as unstable. Those who venture out onto it do so with good motives but will be hurt just the same. That doctrine is false justice.

Ephesians 2:10 tells us that we were created by God to do good works, and that in fact God prepares opportunities for us to do so. We have preset appointments today with people we have never met, in order that we might serve them and the Kingdom of God would be advanced. To do good for others is a drive placed deep in our heart by God.

The false justice movement is not just gospel-light, it's gospel-free. The false justice movement is one that seeks to capitalize on that desire to do good without going so far as to connect Jesus to the works. It is giving a cup of cold water without a mention of his name. It is coordinating with leaders of false religions to do a community service project. It is divorcing the doing of good from the One who is good, which leaves the doer with a false sense of accomplishment and the recipient with a short respite from suffering but no long-term answers. In many ways, it is delaying someone's experience of hell but not actually alleviating the eternal hell to come.

Additionally, it's appeal to our innate motivation to do good can be used to manipulate us and leave us completely detached from the suffering we are trying to address. KONY 2012 was a short film geared towards raising awareness of African warlord Joseph Kony. In just a few days, it took social media platforms by storm, becoming the highest trending TWITTER topic for days. You couldn't turn on the news or open your computer without seeing #Kony2012.

Filmmakers insisted that by making Kony famous, they could catch him and bring him to justice. Incidentally, they also raised nearly $20 million which they earmarked primarily for awareness campaigns. Note: It was an awareness campaign that raised the initial $20 million.

Nowhere in the campaign was their mention of righteousness. It was geared entirely to appeal to the idea that we can band together and do something that really matters. It was part justice, part Tower of Babel. If we can get Kony trending, is there anything we can't do?

Around the world, people contributed. Teens, in particular, were moved to participate. Bake sales were held, fund drives initiated, and more than one father was asked for the credit card to donate $20 to #Kony2012.

How did it all end up? The filmmaker had a short emotional breakdown from the pressure and was found naked, running in San Diego traffic. Kony still roams Africa with his band of child soldiers. And the kids who borrowed dad's credit card? Ask them if they remember who Kony was. In most cases, you'll draw a blank stare.

The devil himself understands that people want to do good things. One of the most subtle deceptions he can utilize is to scratch their itch to do good without allowing their good to have any eternal impact.

• • • • • • • • • • • • • • • • • •

The false justice movement will explode in coming years. Pastors will join hands with imams to build playgrounds, churches will partner with atheist groups to plant flowers, and believers will join with unbelievers to care for the poor.

• • • • • • • • • • • • • • • • • •

The false justice movement will explode in coming years. Pastors will join hands with imams to build playgrounds, churches will partner with atheist groups to plant flowers, and believers will join with unbelievers to care for the poor. The only catch will be that in order to get everyone's participation, the name of Jesus must never be mentioned. This is eternally insignificant. It is actually preparing people for the coming Antichrist who will capitalize on this "do good, godlessly" movement.

Stuart Greaves relays a story about being on a trip to Mexico City, when *"I began to feel his tangible presence resting on me, and I separated myself from the group be to alone and think and pray about the issue of the poor and justice...suddenly the Holy Spirit spoke to me: 'The present social justice movement is preparing the poor of the earth to receive the Antichrist.'"*[15]

Reproductive justice, marriage and equality -- who isn't for treating people equally? Be warned -- justice has become a buzzword that is being co-oped to legitimize everything from infanticide to eco-imperialism, leaving developing countries destitute for the benefit of the developed world.

The nature of God is just and to put forth a false face to justice is right out of the playbook of the Deceiver. Years ago I read a book by a former physic, Johanna Michaelsen, called THE BEAUTIFUL SIDE OF EVIL which woke me up to how many good things the devil does in the world today, even counterfeit miracles. In his book FREEDOM FROM THE SPIRIT OF RELIGION, Dr. Peter Wagner used a university analogy explaining that the University of Hell has a Department of Religion where its minions are taught to use religious devices to maintain the status quo thereby ultimately keeping people from Jesus Christ. Those religious devices include activities which seem good, and in and of themselves they are good. What's bad is when none of it points to Jesus. Those who gravitate toward the social justice movement in the church need to give consideration to how 2 Corinthians 11:14 tells us *"Satan himself masquerades as an angel of light."*

In the doing of short-term good, those who partake in this false justice movement will do long-term damage as they detach the idea of good from righteousness. They will find themselves offering a glass of lemonade to people waiting in line for a guillotine and feeling good about themselves for it.

---

15 Greaves, Stuart. *False Justice; Unveiling the Truth About Social Justice.* (Shippensburg, PA: Destiny Image Publishers, 2012), page 27.

Beloved, I am encouraged because God is raising up a remnant willing to take the narrow path even though no one else is on it. God is raising up a Bride who clings to him rather than just the doctrines about him.

CHAPTER 3

Standing with Israel

Preachers are pretty much ignored by the general population and so my theory is that, every once in a while, when God has something he really wants to say he speaks through late night comedians. Please note that I am being somewhat facetious, but Jay Leno did nail it on the head one night when he said:

With hurricanes, tornados, fires out of control, mud slides, flooding, heat waves and severe thunderstorms tearing up the country from one end to another, and with the threat of bird flu and terrorist attacks...are we sure this is a good time to take God out of the Pledge of Allegiance?[1]

These are increasingly perilous days for the planet.

Most of the time the land we affectionately refer to as the Holy Land is a war zone. Technically, it has almost always been a war zone. There is no doubt these are dreadful days for the people in and around Palestine and we need to pray. Psalm 122:6 says *"Pray for the peace of Jerusalem: May they prosper who love you."* Scripturally, Jerusalem is both a place and a people group. Scripture is quite clear that there is a direct connection between our prosperity (well-being and future security) and our willingness to stand with Israel. If you have any doubt that Israel

---

1   Jay Leno, The Tonight Show, opening monologue, September, 2005.

is central to God's purposes and plans for humanity and the planet consider how historically Israel has been a target of the enemies of God. As strategic as we may think our cool churches are, terrorists are not targeting and blowing up mega-churches in America. They target Israel and those who love her. Genesis 12:3 has never been revoked. There God said to Abraham, "*I will bless those who bless you, and whoever curses you I will curse.*"

Here we come to the third factor fueling the great apostasy. 1 Timothy 4:1 says:

> *The Spirit clearly says that in latter times some will abandon the faith and follow deceiving spirits and doctrines taught by demons.*

This massive falling away will go far beyond mere backsliding and into the realm of betrayal and renouncing core beliefs. In chapter one, I tackled Matthew 24:10-12 which says that many will fall away because their love for God will grow cold. In the last chapter, we looked at how people will fall away because they will be standing on unstable doctrines. I gave my list of six unstable doctrines.[2] Here I'll add a seventh. One of the main reasons people will deliberately deny their faith under the pressure of the end-times is because they refuse to stand with Israel.

> *This massive falling away will go far beyond mere backsliding and into the realm of betrayal and renouncing core beliefs.*

---

2 Cessationism, Pre-Tribulation Dispensationalism, Eternal Security, Universalism, Cheap Grace, and the False Justice Movement.

Israel plays a central role at the end of the age

Revelation 7:4 tells us God will seal—that is, he will keep secure—144,000 from all the tribes of Israel. If God was "done with Israel" as some erroneously assume today, that line would not appear.

Romans 11:8-12, 25-27 is quite clear regarding God's dealings with Israel and what exactly is going on there...

> *God gave them a spirit of stupor, eyes so that they could not see...to this very day...Did they stumble so as to fall beyond recovery? Not at all! Rather, because of their transgression, salvation has come to the Gentiles to make Israel envious. But if their transgression means riches for the world, and their loss means riches for the Gentiles, how much greater riches will their fullness bring!...I do not want you to ignorant of this mystery, brothers so that you may not be conceited: Israel has experienced a hardening in part until the full number of Gentiles is brought in. And so all Israel will be saved, as it written: "The deliverer will come from Zion; he will turn godlessness away from Jacob. And this is my covenant with them when I take away their sins.*

If you have been thinking once we hit the New Testament that God was finished with Israel, you have not actually been reading your New Testament!

Twice in Romans 11 the Apostle Paul says that Israel has not fallen beyond recovery, but that, in fact, Israel is still the "*apple of God's eye.*" In the New Testament, the word "Israel" is used seventy-four times. In seventy-one of those references, it speaks of the nation of Israel. That is ninety-six percent of the time. References to Israel are not synonymous with references to the Church. Perhaps you have heard that Israel rejected God and God replaced them with the Church. It's not true. The Church has been grafted in by God's grace and we ought not boast because Romans 11:18 says Judaism is our root and "*you* (Church) *do not support the root, the root supports you.*"

Replacement Theology

Here I want to add on to the list of unstable doctrines that in times of Great Tribulation will result in a great falling away for those who stand upon them. Replacement Theology is an unstable doctrine. Replacement Theology teaches that when Israel failed, God replaced Israel with the Church. Romans 11:1 says that is blatantly false:

I say then, has God cast away His people? Certainly not!

When something in the Bible is cast away, you never hear of it again. Yet, all the way to the last chapters of the Bible we hear about God's Covenant People Israel.

False doctrine fueled hatred and the Holocaust

Replacement Theology is a false doctrine that, historically, has fueled hatred and holocaust. It will be a very unstable doctrine to be standing on during the pressure of the end-times because we will find ourselves on the wrong side of God and more in alignment with the Antichrist who is determined to do away with God's Covenant People. Satan sees this as a loophole in God's end-time plan. If Israel does not exist, they cannot invite Jesus back and Satan does not get bound for one thousand years.[3]

Replacement Theology has greatly aided his evil efforts. Have you ever wondered before how the holocaust could have happened in Christian Germany? A little history lesson is perhaps in order. The Apostle Paul stressed numerous times in his letters that Gentiles could, though faith in Christ, become full

---

3   Revelation 20:7

participants in God's covenant with Israel without regard to Jewish descent or practice. That's true. But it doesn't take much to turn that truth into a false doctrine that does away with Jews forever.

In the second century, a church father named Justin Martyr wrote that Christians are the "true spiritual Israel."[4] He taught that the Jews—physical Israel—will inherit none of the benefits of the Abrahamic covenants, not even the physical benefits. Everything once promised to the Jews, including the land of Israel itself, will now flow to the Church. Saint Augustine picked up the Replacement Theology doctrine from there and took it to another level by making it official Church doctrine. One historian today says;

> *Augustine's relatively benign attitude toward Jews is rooted in assumptions of supersessionism that would prove deadly...exclusion from God's covenant led to exclusion from Christian society, and then led, too often to exclusion from the human family.*[5]

Did you note the shift from replaced to displaced?

Saint John Chrysostom, the most famous preacher of the patristic period, accused the Jews of deicide and said, *"They are as animals, now unfit for work, ready now for slaughter."* For the next thousand years, Jews faced either conversion or death and the conversion option wasn't always offered.

We all know about Martin Luther—he is one of our heroes—the guy who brought the Church back to the Bible. One would think Martin Luther would have been the perfect guy to challenge antisemitism. However, instead of rejecting Replacement Theology, Luther embraced it. He wrote a treatise called "THE

---

4   Justin Martyr. *Dialog With Trypho* in the Ante-Nicene Fathers. Ed. Alexander Roberts and Jay Donaldson. Peabody, MA: Hendrickson Publishers, 1999.

5   Carroll, James. *Constantine's Sword: The Church and the Jews.* (New York: Houghton Mifflin Books, 2001), 219.

JEWS AND THEIR LIES," calling for Jewish homes to be broken down and destroyed. He said they should be deprived of their prayer books. He said the synagogues should be set on fire.

In 1938, a German bishop named Martin Sasse of Thuringia reprinted that old treatise and circulated it throughout Germany. In the foreword, he noted the "happy coincidence" that:

> *On November 10, 1938, on Luther's birthday, the syna-gogues are burning in Germany.*[6]

Of all the Protestant bishops of Germany, only one, in a confidential letter to Hitler, protested the slaughter of the Jews. We wonder how that could be? The answer is that for more than fifteen hundred years, the Christian churches of Europe taught that when the Jews rejected Christ, the Church replaced them as the true Israel. Historians all agree. Centuries of Christian antisemitism prepared Europe to so readily and enthusiastically embrace Nazi antisemitism.

The end of the story is yet to be written, but I should say that after World War II, the Catholic Church and most Protestant denominations renounced Replacement Theology. But many would say their renouncement went unnoticed in light of their actions and that Replacement Theology is still the doctrine so much of the Church is standing on with regard to the Jews. Granted, there are some shining stars like Corrie Ten Boom, who hid Jews from the Nazis and some key Christian resisters, like Pastors Dietrich Bonhoeffer and Pastor Martin Niemoeller. But many Christians today are still standing on the Replacement Doctrine.

Hitler is dead, but the demonic spirit driving him is still hard at work in the earth.

Here is how all this is relevant to you and me. Hitler is dead, but the demonic spirit driving him is still hard at work in the earth. A few years

---

6   ibid, Carroll, 428.

ago we hosted a special screening of the movie, OBSESSION: RAD-ICAL ISLAM'S WAR WITH THE WEST.[7] Those of you who have seen it heard loud and clear that radical Islam is aligning to eliminate Israel from the face of the earth. This is significant last-days stuff and nations are now choosing sides.

Matthew 25 and the Parable of the Sheep and the Goats is an end-time passage. Both Matthew 24 and 25 comprise Jesus' end-time discourse. Chapter 24 is about the day and hour being unknown. The great falling away is foretold in 24:10. Chapter 25 begins with five of the ten virgins not having sufficient oil to last the night. Chapter 25 ends with the great separation on the last day of the sheep nations and the goat nations (verses 31-46).

The part I want to point out is that the only difference given between the sheep nations and the goat nations is what they did or didn't "*do for the least of these brothers of mine*" (vs. 40). Jesus never called Gentiles his "brothers." This is just one of a number of passages to teach that standing with Israel in the end-times will be the litmus test for the nations of the earth. At the end of the age, God will be looking closely at the degree to which we are source of blessing to Israel.

God's end-time litmus test for the nations

Standing with Israel will become God's litmus test for the nations in the end-times.

> *I will also gather the nations, and...enter into judgment*
> *with them there on account of My people, My heritage*
> *Israel, [I will judge them for all they have done to my*
> *people] whom they scattered among the nations; they*
> *have also divided up my land...multitudes in the valley*

---

7 *Obsession: Radical Islam's War Against The West.* A 77-minute-long DVD documentary produced by Honest Reporting, 2006.

of decision! For the day of the Lord is near in the valley of decision.[8]

This is a passage that tells us we need to make some decisions on this now.

We need to settle these issues now as that Romans passage mentioned earlier warned us not to be *"ignorant of this mystery."* It's not a mystery in that God is not revealing it to anyone. It is a mystery only to those without understanding on the central role of Israel in the end-times. There will come a time when people will scratch their heads on this—even in the Church. *The Jews? Didn't they kill Jesus? Why would I die for them? How are they different from anybody else?*

Many in the Church will fall away at that time because they will not understand how God is using Israel to bring salvation to the world. We need to come to grips with all of this related to Israel so we can be people who rightly interpret the crisis in perfect alignment with God at the end of the age.

The Joel 3 text describes the judgment of the nations on the Day of the Lord and verse 16 says:

The Lord will roar from Zion and thunder from Jerusalem; the earth and the sky will tremble. But the Lord will be a refuge for his people, a stronghold for the people of Israel.

My friends, there is coming a day when you will want to be standing with Israel under divine refuge—not out there with the nations facing the roar of the Lord's judgments. Zechariah 2:8 says, *"He who touches you (Israel) touches the apple of my eye."* Look out! This nation is precious to God.

God deals with nations in relation to how they deal with Israel. History bears witness to this. What a nation does to the

---

8   Joel 3:2, 14

Jewish people, God returns to them. The Egyptians killed Jewish children in the Nile River. Later God sent a plague that killed the firstborn of every house in Egypt without the lamb's blood on the door. This is chronicled in numerous books, most recently in Pastor John Hagee's book, "Jerusalem Countdown."

> *God deals with nations in relation to how they deal with Israel. History bears witness to this. What a nation does to the Jewish people, God returns to them.*

What you do to the Jews will happen to you...Where is the Roman Empire? Where are the Greeks? Where are the Babylonians? Where are the Turks? Where is the Ottoman Empire? Where are Adolf Hitler and his goose-stepping Nazis? They are all footnotes in the boneyard of human history, because they all made a common mistake. They attacked the Jewish people, and God Almighty brought them to nothing...

...in 1984, separating East and West Germany were two ten-feet-high barbed wire fences with a no man's land of one hundred yards filled with machine gun towers and German Shepherd attack dogs...my German tour guide turned to me and fired a question I did not see coming: "Pastor Hagee, why did God allow the Russians to build fences around the German people, with machine guns and attack dogs?"

The answer flashed out of my mouth like lightening: "God allowed the Russians to build barbed-wire fences around the German people to hold you as prisoners with machine guns and German Shepherd attack dogs because the German people did exactly the same thing to the Jews at every death camp. You did this at Dachau and Auschwitz, and for every Jew who died, you will have to answer to God."[9]

Whether we like it or not, Israel is the "*apple of God's eye*" and the root system of God's plan to bring salvation and blessing to the entire earth.

In the late nineteenth century, Queen Victoria asked her Prime Minister this question, "*Mr. Prime Minister, what evidence can you give me for the existence of God?*" The Prime Minister thought for a moment and said, "*The Jew, your majesty.*" Think of that. The survival of the Jewish people is indeed a miracle of God. They survived Pharaoh, Nero, Hitler and all the rest right up to this present age and whether we stand with them at the end of age is a determining factor in whether we survive.

Recently, I was taking in all the depressing news reports—the Middle East on the brink of war, stifling heat waves, the clash between fundamentally opposing belief systems in the stem cell debate. As I listened to the chatter of the media and I found myself wishing for a direct word from God. Wouldn't it be great to have a word from God right about now?

Amazingly, a day or so later, I sensed God did speak through something revealed in the headlines: "MEDIEVAL BOOK OF PSALMS UNEARTHED: FIRST MILLENNIUM MANUSCRIPT, OPEN TO PSALM 83, FOUND IN IRISH MUD BOG."[10] A construction worker was out digging with his back hoe when he spotted something. As it turns out, he spotted a twenty-page, leather bound psalm book that they think dates to around 800-1,000 A.D..

But the amazing part, the part that I believe God wanted to be heard on every news station around the globe, is that it was opened to Psalm 83. Could it be, that when the world needed

9   Hagee, John. *Jerusalem Countdown*. (Lake Mary, FL: Frontline, 2006), 199-200.
10   http://www.cnn.com/2006/WORLD/europe/07/25/ireland.psalms.ap/index.html

a word from God, he orchestrated the discovery of an ancient manuscript in an Irish mud bog?

> *O God, do not kept silent...see how your enemies are astir...with cunning they conspire against your people; they plot against those you cherish. "Come," they say, "Let us destroy them as a nation, that the name of Israel be remembered no more."*

What a coincidence that during these days when, according to news outlets all the world is turning against Israel for overreacting to a kidnapping and radical Islam burns with hatred toward Israel that Psalm 83 would be unearthed?!

My first reaction to this was to think somebody planted it there. It was too perfect. But apparently not, unless we concede that God himself put it there. It is not a stretch for me at all to think he's behind this. I leave things out all the time for Kristen and the kids to see. I cut stuff out and tape it to the television. If I have something I want seen, I will place it on a pillow or leave it lying by the sink. I am not that subtle about it and when we look at Scripture, God is not subtle about Israel.

Psalm 83 is strikingly relevant. Verse five talks about an alliance of Arabs forming against Israel. Verse 12 tells us exactly what this Arab alliance is ultimately after. They said, *"Let us take possession of the pastureland of God."* You know the story. God gave land to Abraham. The borders are given in Genesis 15:18-21:

> *On that day the Lord made a covenant with Abram and said, "To your descendants I give this land, from the River of Egypt to the great river, the Euphrates—the land of the Kenites, Kenizzites, Kadmonites, Hittites, Perizzites, Rephaites, Amorites, Canaanites, Girgashites and Jedusites.*

God gave Abraham ten "lands." These places and people groups mean very little to us, but they are critical to figuring out which lands God gave Abraham.

Land belonging to Abraham's descendants

The descendants of Abraham have a legitimate, historical right to the land and not just "that land." Here's what I mean. The map below is a typical map depicting the borders of land given to Abraham. You can quickly see God gave Abraham more than just the sliver over by the sea, which the nation of Israel calls home today.

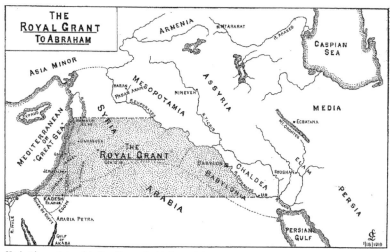

Used with permission of the Rev. Clarence Larkin Estate, P.O. Box 334, Glenside, PA 19038, U.S.A., 215-576-5590

The problem with this map is that we only know where seven of the ten lands given to Abraham are. Three of the ten, the land of the Kenites, Kenizzites and Kadmonites, seem to have disappeared. I just want to be clear that God's Covenant land is far from limited to a little postage stamp the size of New Jersey that we today call Israel. His Covenant People are presently scattered all over the earth—many of them here in the United

States. More descendants of Abraham live in the United States than in Israel.

Sometimes I scratch my head at verses about the New Jerusalem and particularly how its dimensions will not fit in the Holy Land's present boundaries. The dimensions of the New Jerusalem (Revelation 21) are enormous. It is a 1380 mile cube. Plopping that down over the New Jersey-sized nation of Israel as we know it today does not really work. This map gives you an idea of the enormity of the New Jerusalem.

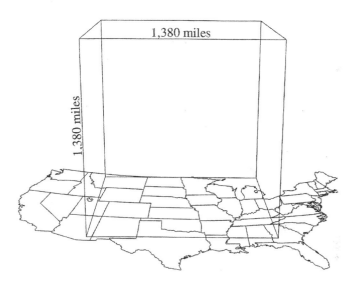

The image is a bit prophetic for me. When I first saw this graphic I had a sense that the burden for the New Jerusalem is resting on America and that the connection between Israel and America goes far beyond being mere political allies. Historically, America has been Israel's best friend in the world, but my sense is the connections between these two will fully be established and recognized at the end of the age.

Out with Replacement Theology, in with Recognition Theology

In my view, the Israel issue is the greatest oversight in the history of Christianity. Hosea 1 is a passage on a previous list I mentioned of one hundred fifty chapters in the Bible relating to the end of the age. Hosea 1:10 tells us the Israelites will be innumerable at the end of the age. *"Yet the Israelites will be like the sand on the seashore, which cannot be measured or counted."*

> *In my view, the Israel issue is the greatest oversight in the history of Christianity.*

We know God made promises to both Isaac and Ishmael. We also know that today there are nearly 400 million Arab people in the various Arab tribes (Ishmaelites). Yet, it's commonly stated that there are somewhere between 12-14 million Jews today (only .002% of the present population of the world). The math here is straight forward and stunning actually: 400 million Ishmaelites today and only 14 million descendants of Isaac. Did God keep his promise to Ishmael but not Isaac or could it be God *did* keep his promise and the descendants of Isaac are a far larger group today than those we presently recognize as Jews?

> *Did God keep his promise to Ishmael but not Isaac or could it be God did keep his promise and the descendants of Isaac are a far larger group today than those we presently recognize as Jews.*

Considering a world population now exceeding six billion people, we are either still a millennium or longer away from the end of the age or God's covenant promise did not come true. Or, more likely, God considers "Israelites" to be a far broader group than merely the Tribe of Judah. Either we are still many, many generations from the end of the age, or there are more blood descendants of Abraham than are presently recognized right now. In fact, that is what we read next in Hosea 1:10. *"In the place where it was said to them, 'You are not my people,' they will be called 'sons of the living God.'"* For reasons known to God, the true identity of masses of people at the end of the age is presently veiled.

The next verse speaks of an end-time reunification of the people of Judah and the people of Israel. *"The people of Judah and the people of Israel will be reunited..."* From the time of the divided kingdom, the designations Judah and Israel ceased to be synonyms either in Scripture or in historical records. These verses in Hosea suggest the identity of the House of Israel will be veiled and not recognized until that latter time when the tribes are reunited.

During the reigns of Jeroboam and Rehoboam, the twelve tribes (thirteen counting Joseph as Ephraim and Manasseh) divided into two kingdoms. Two/three tribes made up the southern kingdom of Judah, ten tribes made up the northern kingdom of Israel. Soon after that we find passages in the Bible that speak of the "Jews" going to war against "Israel."[11] They were separate peoples from this point forward and this is a critical point in correctly understanding Biblical prophecy.

Recognition Theology[12] is a term I coined a few years ago to refer to the unveiling of the identity of millions of the blood descendants of Abraham who presently do not even know who they are. The reason I call this Recognition Theology is because in the providence of God, he has kept this veiled until its forecast

---

11   1 Kings 12:21, 2 Chronicles 11:1

12   Recognition Theology has several related but not-identical sub-streams including Two-House Messianics, British Israelism, Israelite Identity and various others who have interest in the identity of the so-called ten lost tribes of Israel. Recognition Theology vigorously rejects Replacement Theology, Mormon Theology, anti-Semitic or racial supremacy and Aryan race movements and other aberrant racialized theology variations. Recognition Theology celebrates the God who grafts the foreigner into his family and keeps every promise to raise up children of Abraham to be innumerable, a nation and a company of nations, blessing them to be a blessing to all nations.

recognition or unveiling at the end of the age. Recognition Theology is a notable departure from anything presented in the OMEGA COURSE. In chapter one I mentioned that I wrote this book as a follow-up study to the OMEGA COURSE. Though nothing with regard to Recognition Theology conflicts with anything presented in the OMEGA COURSE, I want to be up front and make it clear that this is a notable departure. Yet, I present it to you because it is central to understanding Israel, who she is, and who is for and against her at a critical time in the unveiling of God's plan for the earth. As Mike Bickle does repeatedly in the OMEGA COURSE, I also implore you to not take me at my word, but rather search these things out in Scripture yourself. If what I put forth here does not align with Scripture in your estimation, reject it.

Recognition Theology contends that numerous nations and peoples, including America, are absolutely identifiable and recognizable in Bible prophecy,[13] archeology, genographic migration studies and haplotype studies.[14] The promise to the descendants of Abraham was that they would grow into "*a nation and company of nations.*"[15] No doubt the nation Israel is that nation. However, as that verse clearly indicates, the descendants of Abraham were not limited to that nation. We know that Israel today is by and large made up of descendants of the tribe of Judah and Benjamin, as those were the two tribes that returned from the exile. Interestingly there is a company of approximately one hundred "Christian" nations today, most of whom support Israel.

---

13 If this interests you please read a superb article by my friend Steven M. Collins called *The United States of America in Biblical Prophecy* available here - http://stevenmcollins.com/html/usa_in_prophecy.html I also highly recommend his four books which deal exhaustively with this topic – *Volume One: The Origins and Empires of Ancient Israel; Volume Two: Israel's Lost Empires; Volume Three: Parthia – The Forgotten Ancient Superpower and It's Role In Biblical History* and *Volume Four: Israel's Tribes Today.*

14 Entrine, Jon. *Abraham's Children: Race, Identity, and the DNA of the Chosen People.* Grand Central Publishing, 2007.

15 Genesis 35:11

In 586 B.C., when the First Temple was destroyed and twelve tribes were exiled from the Holy Land, it is estimated that they numbered around ten million. During the time of Nehemiah and Ezra, only a remnant returned (43,000 families which may number approximately 250,000 people). The remnant was mainly, though not exclusively, from the tribes of Judah and Benjamin. Millions of blood descendants of Abraham, almost entirely from the other ten tribes, assimilated into the surrounding pagan nations. Over the last twenty-five hundred years these covenant people migrated and literally populated a number of the nations on earth today. At present, only God knows exactly who and where they are, but we are certain that his promise for those people is irrevocable.

Imagine that millions of the blood descendants of Abraham, those we now consider the lost ten tribes, assimilated into pagan nations and migrated far from home. They did not vanish or disappear from the face of the earth, nor did the unconditional and irrevocable (Abrahamic Covenant) promises of God for their future get forfeited or canceled. God knows their identity in him even though they have no recognition of it. Jesus and his disciples were sent to the lost sheep of Israel.[16] Their whereabouts were not unknown. They were lost in a spiritual sense. These tribes and people groups have since increased into many large nations—innumerable, exactly as prophesied —increasing even more by adopting many "foreigners" into their national (covenant) family. And precisely as the Bible predicted, the descendants of David still sit on the thrones of nations[17] and possess the gates of their enemies.[18]

God's promises to the descendants of David came true. They did and still do sit on the thrones of nations and historically they have and still do control the main geo-political gates of the

---

16   Matthew 10:6, 15:24.
17   Jeremiah 33:17.
18   Genesis 24:60.

world; Gibraltar, the Suez Canal, Singapore, and Hong Kong to name a few. In the fifteenth century, Mary Queen of Scots traced her royal lineage back to King David and this was made plainly evident in the Scottish Declaration of Independence, also called the DECLARATION OF ARBROATH, which expressly states:

> *Most Holy Father and Lord, we know and from the chronicles and books of the ancients we find that... the Scots... journeyed from Greater Scythia by way of the Tyrrhenian Sea and the Pillars of Hercules, and dwelt for a long time in Spain... Thence they came, twelve hundred years after the people of Israel crossed the Red Sea, to their home in the west where they live today...[19]*

It is apparent that five centuries ago the Scots considered themselves blood descendants of Abraham and were aware of the specific migration routes that brought them to their new homeland.

Queen Victoria, the Duke and Duchess of Kent, the abdicated King Edward the 8th, the Duke of Windsor, and notably, Winston Churchill recognized vast populations of Israelites (blood descendants of Abraham) as distinguished from those presently identified as Jews or Judahites.

Of the various other notable examples, my favorite is President Harry S. Truman. That historic afternoon of May 14, 1948, State Department officials informed President Truman the new nation would be called *Israel*, which surprised him, as he noted that he thought they would name it *Judea* after the people, not Israel after the land.[20] Obviously he was aware that what we call *Israel* today is mainly populated by the tribe of *Judah*.

---

19 *The Scottish Declaration of Independence* reprinted in *The Declaration of Arbroath*, The National Trust for Scotland, 1970.

20 The May 14, 2007 issue a NEWSWEEK included an exclusive book excerpt entitled; "*A Case for Courage*." The excerpt was from a chapter called "*I Am Cyrus*" about Truman and the birth of Israel from leading presidential historian Michael

This is an enormous and fascinating study, potentially permanently changing how we read the Bible. However, to continue on this will detract from the point of this chapter. Many will fall away at the end of the age because of an animosity toward Israel, fed by a total lack of awareness as to how this nation and company of nations fit into God's end-time plan.

Beschloss's book, *Presidential Courage: Brave Leaders and How They Changed America 1789-1989.*

CHAPTER 4

Mad at God

Ever been mad at God? Be honest. Many in the world today are mad at God. That will only increase in the end-times as the world becomes an increasingly hostile place. How could a loving God pour out bowls of wrath? Matthew 24:10 says that in the last days many will be offended by God and fall away from the faith. It is one of the main factors fueling the great apostasy of the end-times. A common human reaction in hard times is to curse the God who supposedly should not allow calamities.

Part of my ministerial training in seminary was called CPE or Clinical Pastoral Education. It was a six-month program where I served as a hospital chaplain in downtown Chicago. Twice a week I did a twenty-four hour shift in the hospital, visiting the sick and dying. I saw, on average, six deaths a day. Some days there were more.

Early on, my supervisor warned me to be careful when I walked into a room wearing my chaplain's coat. He said, "*Many times when this bad stuff happens to people they get mad at God and you represent God.*" He was right. On a number of occasions, people took the opportunity to say to me what they thought of God. Pain hurts and hurting people can hurt people and quickly develop offenses with God.

In my capacity as a city police chaplain, I informed a woman that her son was found dead. After the initial wave of devastation seemed to subside, I asked if she would mind if I offered a prayer. Every feeling in her heart seemed to shoot out her eyes right at me when she clenched her teeth and said, *"Yes, I do mind if you offered a prayer."*

She later apologized to me and tried to clarify that her anger was not with me but rather with, *"the one I work for."* What you would have said? My response was something like, *"It's okay. I understand. I see it a lot when I deliver this kind of news."* All the way home I tried to think of something better I could have said. At least she did not hit me. On one death notification a lady pounded away on me when I broke the bad news. Others hit the closest thing to them.

Several years ago my son, Thomas, and I went to Kiev, Ukraine to support a pastor friend of mine during a key anniversary of his church. One of our translators was a gal from Moscow named Valaria. She told us her testimony of being a Russian Jew who accepted Christ only eighteen months earlier. But a few days later she made a comment about her parents being atheists. I said, *"I thought you said your family was Jewish?"* She said, *"They are, but most of them gave up any belief in God after the holocaust. Then we lived through the Chernobyl nuclear accident."* Chernobyl is only twenty miles upstream from Kiev. The Chernobyl fallout was four hundred times greater than that of Hiroshima. Valaria said, *"Chernobyl made it even harder to believe there is a God."*

In hard times, people seem to do one of two things; cling to God or curse God, they either run to Him or they reject Him. Some vacillate between the two extremes as they sort it all out. It is similar to a child who cries after a spanking from his parents only to be consoled by them just a moment later. But in the end-times, it will be one or the other. People will either turn toward him or turn against him.

The end-times will be hard times for the human race and the entire planet

Matthew 24:6-29 captures the distress of those days. *"You will hear of wars and rumors of wars, but see to it that you are not alarmed."* God is very concerned that we understand and rightly interpret all that will unfold in the end. Those without understanding will turn on God during this time rather than turn to him. Jesus is greatly concerned for our reaction to the difficulty of the end-times. He wants us to know:

> *Such things must happen, but the end is still to come. Nation will rise against nation, and kingdom against kingdom. There will be famines and earthquakes in various places. All these are the beginning of birth pains.... For then there will be great distress, unequaled from the beginning of the world until now—and never to be equaled again. If those days had not been cut short, no one would survive, but for the sake of the elect those days will be shortened. Immediately after the distress of those days 'the sun will be darkened, and the moon will not give its light; the stars will fall from the sky, and the heavenly bodies will be shaken." At that time, the sign of the Son of Man will appear in the sky, and all the nations of the earth will mourn. They will see the Son of Man coming on the clouds of the sky, with great power and great glory. And he will send his angels with a loud trumpet call, and they will gather the elect from the four winds from one end of the earth to the other...*

It is difficult to imagine all the nations of the earth going into mourning. We saw it on a small scale with the Asian tsunami of 2004 or more recently in the 2011 earthquake and subsequent tsunami in Japan. We went though something similar in the United States after September 11, 2001. But this says there will be such a crescendo of calamity across the entire planet that every nation will be profoundly affected. More details are out-lined in the OMEGA COURSE, but it's perhaps enough here to list the four sources of pressure during the Tribulation.

1) The Wrath of God is poured out on the rebellious

Revelation 14:10 says, "...*the wrath of God, which is poured out full strength...*" (NKJV). Oh my, what does "*full strength*" mean to the God of Genesis one? This will come in three succes-sive waves of judgment; seven seals, seven trumpets, and final-ly, the seven bowls of wrath.[1] Many without understanding will have no point of reference for this and will quickly turn against God and conclude that he is not fair or good.

2) The Rage of Satan against the Saints

The second source of pressure during the Tribulation will come from the rage of Satan and the Antichrist against the Saints. The enemies of God will retaliate against the Bride, which will result in persecution.

3) Evil people acting without restraint

The third source of pressure will be the actions of evil people against each other. The Bible says "*the restrainer*"[2] will be lifted from the earth, resulting in people following their evil desires to the fullest. There are many passages that talk about the rise in lawlessness and murder in the end-times as the "*restrainer*" is removed. My view is the restrainer is natural government which loses control on societies during this difficult time in human history.

---

1   Revelation 6 records the seal judgments against the kingdom of darkness. Revelation 8-9 records the trumpet judgments against the Antichrist's empire. Revelation 15-16 records the bowl judgments, which destroy the evil infrastructures of society.
2   2 Thessalonians 2:6-10

4) Natural cataclysms

The fourth source of pressure is convulsions in nature (earthquakes, drought, etc.). We are told in Matthew 24 these things will be as birth pangs. As birth pangs means they will happen more and more frequently. It is not difficult to see how many will become deeply offended at God and fall away. God will seem too harsh or too far removed from it all.

As the righteousness of God comes forth in the earth in the last days, God will seem unjust and unfair. People will be unable to reconcile how God could be both all-powerful (able to intervene and stop a calamity) with the fact that he is also all-loving. If he was indeed all-loving then surely he would have stopped it. It rattles people today when I say things like: apparently God loves righteousness more than he loves people. In the Bible, every time God was faced with a choice between righteousness and people, he choose righteousness. He even chose righteousness over his own Son. We don't like to hear that but we need to think it through. Hell would not exist if God chose people over righteousness.

Someone once asked R.C. Sproul why bad things happen to good people. Sproul's answer was to say "that only happened once and he volunteered for it." The question when bad things happen is not "how could God let them die?" The question is "Why does he let us all live?"

Friends, God is just and he's justified. God is not mean nor is he cruel. He takes no pleasure in the death of the wicked (Ezekiel 33:11), and by the way, we shouldn't either. From a meta-perspective, God is good and only up to good. Even so, it's a bad day for those who are bad when God makes things right. If God isn't just then God is not good. Many today are crying out for justice--- *How long Lord until you avenge our blood?* We need to think about this: if we are praying for justice we are praying for targeted judgment. If we are praying for mercy, and we should be praying for mercy, we are praying God would relent.

These are tough theological concepts to sort through because at a definitional level, justice and mercy should cancel each other out. Justice is when we get what we deserve. Mercy is when we don't. My contention in this chapter is that Christians today are very superficial in their knowledge of God and decades of theology-lite from the pulpit has produced people resting theologically on sand. When the storm comes, only those on a solid theological foundation will remain.

There is both an ouch and an awe in drawing near to God

The time to pursue the knowledge of God is now and what you will discover is that there is both an awe and an ouch in coming near this One who is holy, righteous and just. Many today have a very low view of God and a very high view of humanity. Today people think God is one of us and we are all pretty good and so when something bad happens we can't accept that he had anything to do with it because, after all, God is like us and we are pretty good and we'd never do those things to people. We get a different picture in the Bible. The Bible puts forth a very high view of God as holy and righteous and a low view of man in our rebellion and depravity of heart.

Many today have a very low view of God and a very high view of humanity... we get a different picture in the Bible.

These are enormous issues we need to grapple with and settle today. Romans 11:22 says *"Consider therefore the kindness and sternness of God..."* The kindness message is preached widely today. Everyone loves the kindness message: God loves you, he's good and he's always in a good mood, he's forgiving, he'd never throw a stone and he certainly wouldn't send a storm. No one wants to hear the sternness message. Even some of my favorite ministers today are saying things like "Jesus never created a storm, he only calmed them." That's sounds wonderful but it's pathetic theology.

Colossians 1:15-17 tells us Jesus sustains every atom by his Word. "*By him all things were created: things in heaven and on earth... all powers- he is the sustainer of all things... he is before all things... in him all things hold together.*" When things come apart, are we to believe he lost control? No. The night Jesus stilled the storm the people who saw it said "*What kind of man is this? Even the wind and the waves obey him?*" Previously he was sleeping in the boat. *Or was he?*

According to Colossians it was Jesus who, in his peace was setting up a storm scenario to demonstrate his power over wind and waves and to point to himself as the source of peace. While the disciples were saying, no, no, no to the storm, Jesus was apparently saying yes, yes, yes. It is very evident that his "yes" had limitations. Up until the point where the storm served his purposes he commanded it to stop. No earthquake comes, no tornado strikes a town and no tsunami wipes out a coastline unless God signs off on it.

A popular evangelical blogger, Rachel Held Evans, has written numerous articles after natural disasters basically making the case God has nothing to with them. Pastor John Piper took issue with her comments after the Joplin tornado and tweeted: "Rachel Held Evans lives in a world where innocent people just get caught in the machinery and God is terribly sorry about it."

It is bizarre to sing "Savior, he can move the mountains" while contending God would never ever have anything to do with an earthquake. Rachel Held Evans is not alone in evangelicalism in putting forth this notion that God went through some sort of personality change in the New Testament. Paul rejected that notion and again, told us to give consideration to both the kindness and sternness of God. God is revealed as simultaneously kind and stern in both the Old and New Testaments.

One of the early Christian heretics was a man named Marcion. He rejected the Hebrew Bible and the God of the Old Testament. He was a "New Testament Only" Christian and there are many of those today. Marcionism is alive and well today in evangelical Christianity, as is deism. Evangelical deists assert that God can't and doesn't intervene today. Contemporary evangelical Marcionites purport Jesus isn't like his grumpy old Father.

Here is what is true: Jesus is the revelation of the Father, the exact representation of his being. When you look at Jesus you are looking at the God of the targeted plagues on Egypt. In his sovereignty, Jesus still commands wind and waves.

Psalm 135:6 says...

The Lord does whatever pleases him, in the heavens and on the earth, in the seas and all their depths.

Ever wonder what God is doing today in the depths of the seas? He's doing what pleases him and what pleases him is what accomplishes his purposes. Among other things, on occasion God today is in the depth of the sea shifting plates such that sleeping nations are shaken. The Psalm continues...

He makes the clouds rise from the ends of the earth; he sends lightening with the rain and brings wind out of the storehouses. He struck down the firstborn of Egypt,... he sent signs and wonders into your midst, O Egypt...

Now read that same verse realizing that theologically we can place Jesus' name right there...

JESUS makes the clouds rise from the ends of the earth; JESUS sends lightening with the rain and brings wind out of the storehouses. JESUS struck down the firstborn of Egypt,... JESUS sent signs and wonders into your midst, O Egypt...

To drive a wedge between the unity of the Trinity is a grave error. To drive a wedge between the Old and New Testament is a grave error. *God is the same yesterday, today and forever.*

In my course on natural disasters which I've dubbed "GOD AND NATURE AND THE NATURE OF GOD," I work through these issues. In the middle of a session when I was asserting no tsunami wipes out a coastline unless God signs off on it, someone raised their hand and said emphatically *"NO, the Lord was NOT in the earthquake and he was NOT in the wind."* This is of course a reference to Elijah's encounter with God in the still small voice (1 Kings 19:11). My reply was to ask, where did God limit himself to only speaking from now on in a still gentle whisper? Just because he wasn't speaking in that earthquake and wind doesn't mean he never uses those means to send a message to us.

In fact, Nahum 1:3 expressly says *"His way is in the whirlwind and the storm, and the clouds are the dust of his feet."* In other words, what we see when we see weather is the dust kicked up from where he just walked. In Jonah 1:4 we read *"God hurled a violent storm on the sea."* His intent wasn't to break up the ship. His intent was to get the rebellious prophet out of that boat and back into a place of obedience. We know judgment begins with the house of God and that is what we see here: God sends storms to prophets before he sends them to cities. Do you have a theology for a God who hurls violent storms at people? If you don't, the unfolding of the Book of Revelation will be a significant stumbling block to you. Those who can't comprehend God won't tolerate him during this period.

Now to the part where it gets exciting to me. All authority in heaven and on earth was given to Jesus and we now rule and reign with him in high places. Correct? Correct. We also know God delegated weather-making authority to Satan, in some limited fashion, at least in the case of the calamities that came on the household of Job. We also know he uses third party agents in judgment, pagan nations and probably also he lifts the restraining order off the Evil One and the result is his judgment and people get what they deserve. The point is God delegates weather making authority. Who besides Satan walks in the limited and delegated authority of God on earth today? Clearly, the Church.

Do you have a theology for Christians commanding storms and for the praying prophetic church of the last days to walk in weather-making authority? If we believe, and I hope we don't, that God has nothing to do with the weather today then why would we pray for clear skies for a wedding or for rain in drought? Every farmer in our nation prays for rain but very few have any idea how any of this works theologically or our role in it.

Micah 7:15 says it will be at the end of the age as it was during the Exodus. *"As in the days when you came out of Egypt, I will show you my wonders."* Those wonders included a series of targeted judgments in the form of natural disasters released through Moses. In the last days the righteous will be more than just victims and observers, they will be participants. God is raising up people today who are growing up into the stature of men like Moses who use their limited and delegated authority to tear down end-time Pharaohs. He's raising up end-time Elijah's - men just like us as it says in James 5:17 - who pray with such authority that rains stop and start with their prayers. You say, Really? Can good people really pray for bad things to happen on earth?

The answer is *yes* and that doesn't make us bad people. Mike Bickle frequently says: God uses the least severe means to reach the greatest number of people, at the deepest level of love. Like he used Moses and Elijah, God will use praying and prophetic people in the days to come to agree with his heart and trust his judgments. There is a reason Joel 2:31 calls it the coming *"great and terrible Day of the Lord."* It will be great as God breaks in and it will be terrible. This chapter is about the fact that many will not know God nor will they be attuned to the disposition of his heart at various moments and be able to discern whether now is a time to pray for justice or mercy, or both... *in judgment, remember mercy* (Habakkuk 3:2).

These will be days when good will look evil and evil will look good. God's judgments are not evil though many will interpret them as such. Romans 14:6 says; *"Don't allow what you consider good to be spoken of as evil."* This is already happening. Those who are trying to make a case for marriage being between one man and one woman are looked on as intolerant, extreme, judgmental, dangerous and narrow-minded. Here in South Dakota, we are working to stop the legalized killing of the unborn and the other side is printing bumper stickers that say, "SD HATES RAPE VICTIMS."

Those who stand for good are written off as bad. This is just a taste of what is to come. When righteousness comes down on the earth in the end-times, many people will see it as a bad thing. They will think God needs to lighten up. They will fight him and resist him. The Antichrist will be far more appealing to many with his message of tolerance and his false peace.

Many people who have no spiritual understanding will fall for a counterfeit peace. God will seem like the problem and this slick, subtle one will emerge with deceiving solutions. I want to ask where your heart will be during these times. Have you given any thought to your threshold for tribulation? Is there a point at which you would say, *"Enough with God. He's too extreme!"*

I have a pastor friend whose daughter was diagnosed with a fatal form of Multiple Sclerosis. The news shook him off his foundation for a short season. As he tells the story, he flat out said to God:

> *God, I came here to make it hard to go to hell from Birmingham. I came here to serve you. But if this is some sort of counter-attack on my family...God, if you*

are making me choose here between my daughter and Birmingham, Birmingham can go to hell. I choose her.

This guy is leading one of the fastest growing churches in America. The end of the story is that the Lord ended up healing his daughter after he surrendered himself to serving God no matter the cost. But I tell the story to make an additional point.

Hard times will increasingly polarize the people of the earth

We ought to give great consideration to the story of Job and particularly how he and his wife had very different reactions to their family's suffering. At the beginning of the story Job is wealthy and prosperous, but Satan is given some access to Job's life. Actually, Satan is allowed to tamper with everything in Job's life, but he may not kill him.

In verse fourteen of chapter one, messengers start running up to Job. The first one came to report that the Sabeans attacked and carried off his oxen and donkeys and killed his servants. Verse 16 says:

While he was still speaking, another messenger came and said, "The fire of God fell from the sky and burned up the sheep and the servants...While he was still speaking, another messenger came and said, "The Chaldeans formed three raiding parties and swept down on your camels and carried them off. They put the servants to the sword...While he was still speaking, yet another messenger came and said, "Your sons and daughters were feasting and drinking wine at the oldest brother's house, when suddenly a mighty wind swept in from the desert and struck the four corners of the house. It collapsed on them and they are dead..."

This is the sort of succession and amplification of suffering that we see forecast for the end-times, not only on an individual scale, but on a global scale. In my book, MOMENTUM: GOD'S EV-ER-INCREASING KINGDOM,[3] I conclude with a chapter titled, *"Escalation in the End Times"* and develop this crescendo of suffering.

God will use the tribulation fires of the end-times to purify the Church and ready us to rule and reign with him throughout eternity. But many who are now faithful, will not stay with him because deep offense will take root in their hearts.

I have a long-term friendship with a man who has no interest to ever step into a church. He is a good person. He cries when he sees and hears of children dying, but says he *"doesn't want to go to heaven because he's afraid he'd punch the Big Guy in the nose for standing by while children die."* He says, *"Any god, or anybody for that matter, who kills kids or stands idly by while they are raped and abused isn't someone I'd want to spend much time with, let alone an eternity."*

Job and his wife were in the intensity of those moments. But in verses 20-22, Job models for us a faithful response to the fires of suffering:

> *At this, Job got up and tore his robe and shaved his head. Then he fell to the ground in worship and said: "Naked I came from my mother's womb, and naked I will depart. The Lord gave and the Lord has taken away; may the name of the Lord be praised." In all this, Job did not sin by charging God with wrongdoing.*

With regard to his relationship with God, Job was a hell-or-high-water person. We must become hell-or-high-water people if we aim to stay the course to the end. My favorite line out of the Book of Job is, *"Though he slay me, yet will I hope in him... indeed, this will turn out for my deliverance..."*[4] Job realized that, *"indeed, this will turn out for my deliverance."*

---

3   Hickey, Steve. *Momentum: God's Ever-Increasing Kingdom.* (Lake Mary, FL: Creation House Press, 2009), 149ff.
4   Job 13:15-16

Offense is inevitable apart from understanding

Job had an understanding of God that transcended every circumstantial thing. It is evident that he saw past life in this world to the spiritual reality of God and His plans. He did not charge God with wrongdoing because he knew that God does not do wrong.

His wife apparently did not understand that. We can empathize with her situation. She just lost her whole family and then her husband broke out with painful sores from the *"soles of his feet to the top of his head."* She was probably still fixated on a line in chapter one where the messenger said it was the *"fire of God"* that fell on their lives.

In chapter two, she immediately turned against God. In verse 8, while Job was sitting among the ashes, scraping himself with a piece of broken pottery, his wife said to him:

> *Are you still holding on to your integrity? Curse God and die! He replied, "You are talking like a foolish woman* [a person without understanding—one who doesn't get it]. *Shall we accept good from God, and not trouble?" In all this, Job did not sin in what he said.*

Job's wife basically said, *"Job, come on. Why hold on to a sentimental belief in a loving God when so much of life conspires against that belief?"*

People sort out suffering and tribulation in a variety of ways. Elie Wiesel, a Jewish writer from an earlier generation, began with strong faith in God, but saw that faith vaporize in the gas furnaces of the holocaust. When he came face to face with history's most horrific unfairness, he concluded God must not exist.

Another Jewish author came to a different conclusion. Rabbi Harold Kushner watched his son die of the disease Progeria, which accelerates the aging process. Rabbi Kushner concluded, *"even God has a hard time keeping chaos in check"* and that

"*God is a God of justice and not of power.*" He wrote, "*God is as frustrated as anyone else by the evil on this planet, but lacks the power to change it.*"

Another category of people flatly deny these dilemmas and insist the world is fair. Job's friends fit into this category. They insisted that the world does run according to fixed, regular laws and that good people will prosper and evil people will fail.

Life isn't fair, but God is

Revelation 16:5-7 tells us that when the bowls of wrath are coming forth, an angel says, "*You are just in these judgments… Yes, Lord God Almighty, true and just are your judgments.*" It is important that we do not confuse God with life. If we develop a relationship with God apart from our circumstances, we will be able to hang on when the difficulties of life come crashing in. We, like Job, can trust the Lord despite the unfairness of life. The cliché is true—*I know not what the future holds, but I know who holds the future.* In Job's words, "*Though he slay me, yet will I hope in him…indeed this will turn out for my redemption*"! In chapter 19:25-29, Job says:

> *I know that my Redeemer lives, and that in the end he will stand upon the earth. And after my skin has been destroyed, yet in my flesh I will see God. I myself will see him with my own eyes—I, and not another. How my heart yearns within me! "If you say, 'How will we hound him, since the root of the trouble lies in him, you should fear the sword yourselves; for wrath will bring punishment by the sword, and then you will know that there is judgment."*

In the last days, many will not understand times of tribulation correctly. Many will "*lean on their own understanding.*" That comes from Proverbs 3:5, which says, "*trust in the Lord*

with all your heart and lean not on your own understanding."
Your own understanding will be an increasingly unstable wall to
rest your weight on during the pressure of the end-times. Most
of the book of Job is a transcript of human attempts to understand on their own. His friends all chimed in with their ideas.

God let this pontification and bloviating continue for several
chapters but in chapter 38, God broke in and reoriented (actually
rebuked) their limited thinking about the realities of life:

> *Who is this that darkens my counsel with words without
> knowledge? Brace yourself like a man...Where were
> you when I laid the earth's foundation? Tell me if you
> understand. Who marked off its dimensions? Surely
> you know!...Who shut up the sea behind doors when it
> burst forth from the womb...when I said, "This far you
> may come and no farther; here is where your proud
> waves halt?"*

God was essentially saying, *"Can you even grasp a fraction
of what is really going on this world?"* He continued on like this
for three chapters.

Job interjected a sentence now and then, but only to say, *"I
am unworthy—how can I reply to you? I put my hand over my
mouth."* (40:4). After Job said that, God started right in again.
"Brace yourself like a man...Would you discredit my justice?"
(verses 7-8). It's not that God is being unreasonable here. These
verses are a rebuke to our limited understanding. Many will
fall away in the end-times because they will process the crisis
through their own fallen lenses and charge God with wrongdoing.

Twice in the New Testament Jesus is called the *"Rock of
Offense."*[5] Some translations render this—he's the *"rock that
makes men fall."* Jesus will cause many to stumble. In Matthew

---

5   Romans 9:33; 1 Peter 2:8

21, Jesus told his followers that he is, "*the stone the builders rejected.*" Right after he was called the rock of offense, he said:

He who falls on this stone will be broken to pieces, but he on whom it falls will be crushed. [6]

The bottom line is either that we fall on the Rock, or the Rock falls on us. One will ultimately be the most secure foundation under us in storms. The other will crush us to powder.

---

6   Matthew 21:44

CHAPTER 5

Halfheartedness

Second only to al-Qaeda, Hezbollah frequently makes international headlines for their insidious involvement in acts of terrorism. At this time support for Hezbollah is growing daily, but I was surprised to learn that Hezbollah is really only 100,000-200,000 strong. In fact, they only have 600-1,000 active fighters in their military wing. They own a satellite television company and have eleven members occupying seats on the Lebanese parliament. How is it that only 1,000 fighters have become such a frustration to the rest of the civilized world?

I find it interesting that Hezbollah means "Party of God" and that it was started by a group of clerics who were sold out to the teachings of the late Ayatollah Khomeini. They have only existed since the early 1980s. Today they are the leading Shiite Islamic resistance group in the Middle East. An article I read said they can be described in one word—passionate, as they are wholeheartedly devoted to furthering Islamic domination.

Contrast all that with the fact that 32% of the world is "Christian." Rick Warren likes to say that, *"the Christian Church is the only truly global organization."*[1] We have 1.973 billion members strategically positioned on every continent. Nearly every nation

---

1   Lindy Lowry's 2010 online article… *Rick Warren on the AIDS Crisis*. http://www.churchleaders.com/outreach-missions/outreach-missions-articles/139413-rick-warren-on-outreach.html

and government is infiltrated at some level. There is a witness in every legitimate occupation. The Lord Jesus has agents and ambassadors most everywhere. So, if you were given just one word to describe this global, true "party of God" we call the Body of Christ, what one word would you use?

Before I share the word I picked I will give a disclaimer. The description probably only fits the Body of Christ here in the West. Halfhearted is the word I pick to describe the Body of Christ in the West. Amos 5 contains a sobering prophetic account of the coming Day of the Lord. Chapter 6 tells us that it will be hard on a certain group. "W*oe to those at ease in Zion…*"

Some translations say, "W*oe to you who are complacent or smug.*" The following are synonyms for halfhearted; lackadaisical, distracted, lax, laissez-faire, uncommitted, unenthusiastic, without passion. Granted, comparing Hezbollah with the Global Church is hardly an apples-to-apples comparison, but both do purport to be the "party of God" and both do live under a mandate to bring the entire earth under the dominion of its Lord. But at present, one has passion and the other has barely a remnant at prayer meetings. The point here is not to pile on guilt. The point is to better prepare us to endure the end-times.

It will take your whole heart to sustain you through the whole Tribulation

We cannot fight this with one hand tied behind our back. The pressure of the end-times will be so great on the Body of Christ that many will not be able to stand up under it. They will have no threshold for suffering and those in the Body without sincere love for the Lord will have nothing to fuel their fight.

Love brings out extraordinary stamina. It is an unquenchable flame. Whenever I preach on apostasy and the great falling away, people start wrestling with the fear. *Will I fall away? How do I know I'll be able to endure until the end?* But let me assure you apostasy is not an option for those who love the Lord. Song of Solomon 8:6 assures us:

> *Love brings out extraordinary stamina.*

Love is invincible facing danger and death. Passion laughs at the terrors of hell. The fire of love stops at nothing—it sweeps everything before it. Flood waters can't drown love, torrents of rain can't put it out. [THE MESSAGE]

But we have to consider that hell *will* dominate those whose devotion to the Lord is only halfhearted.

Daniel 11:34 says, *"many who are not sincere"* will join those who fall away. Heading into the end-times with halfhearted devotion to the Lord would be like heading out across Death Valley with only a half tank of gas. The Parable of the Ten Virgins in Matthew 25 reveals that five of the ten will not have oil sufficient to last the night. The oil is our present level of yearning for the Lord. This chapter is about pursuing the Lord in love. It is about the importance of being his lovesick Bride.

My wife tells a story of a time when someone in the church deeply hurt us. This went way beyond the daily drama of life together in the Body of Christ. Our hearts were injured. She had a dream that took place on a Civil War battlefield. As she looked down, she saw a cannonball-sized hole in her chest. She cried out to God that her heart was gone. The Lord spoke back to her saying, *"How could your heart be gone? You gave it to me."* Those who have heard her tell this story know the effect that word had on us. We can endure everything that happens here as long as our hearts are secure with him.

One night our family sat down to watch the movie FEVER PITCH, starring Drew Barrymore as Lindsey and Jimmy Fallon as Ben. It is both a love story and a baseball movie. Lindsey spends the entire movie trying to figure out if Ben loves Lindsey or if Ben loves the RED SOX. It is a movie about a love triangle, only with a twist. Instead of it revolving around three people, this story revolves around 28—a man, a woman and a major league baseball team. Ben has to make up his mind what is more important to him, Lindsey or his RED SOX. It is a movie about the ultimately captivating a previously divided heart.

In Psalm 86:11, King David prayed for an "*undivided heart.*" He apparently realized that God will not be part of a love triangle. Take out a piece of paper the next time you have a quiet moment and draw out a love triangle. It's you, God and what? Or maybe three is not enough. Maybe your heart's devotion could be better mapped out with a hexagon, or an octagon. Look at your heart to see if indeed your whole heart is devoted to the Lord.

The movie is cute and lighthearted, but this is far from a trivial topic in the Word of God. In fact, this will be the very thing that gets sorted out in the end-times. It will increasingly become one or the other. Either our hearts are his, or they are devoted to another. What we see in Scripture is not a game, but very much a love story. The issue of love will be sorted out in the end-times as our heart's true devotion will be exposed.

When I read the end-time Scriptures, I have trouble imagining the extreme tribulation. But I do not have trouble seeing how halfhearted people will start dropping off like flies. That is why this first point is so important. It will take your whole heart to sustain you through the whole Tribulation. The number one thing these particular "apostates" lack is the number one thing God has always asked for.

Wholehearted devotion

Jesus said this is the first and greatest commandment, "*Love the Lord your God will all your heart.*" That phrase is repeated throughout the Bible making it clear what God is after. One of the memorable lines to me in the OMEGA COURSE is this. "*God's purpose in sending judgment is to remove everything that hinders love.*" When we think of the end-times, we tend to think only of the horrible things that will happen.

But consider that the driving force behind the trauma of the end-times is not so much wrath as it is love. God is angry at what hinders his love from reaching the world. Satan has slithered in between God and the objects of this love for too long. The end-times process is God's removal of that which hinders love. 2 Peter 3 discusses the coming Day of the Lord and how the elements of earth will be, "*destroyed by fire.*" God will remove all these things that have vied for our devotion.

In the end-times, his great jealousy will be satisfied. In Exodus 34:14, Moses warns the people leaving Egypt before they enter the new land:

> *Break down their altars, smash their sacred stones and cut down their Asherah poles. Do not worship any other god, for the Lord, whose name is Jealous, is a jealous God.*

Deuteronomy 4:24 says, "*God is a consuming fire, a jealous God.*"

My wife, Kristen, had a blog she dubbed MIDNIGHT CRY, where she wrote about prayer and wholehearted devotion to the Lord. In one of her posts, she wrote about Oprah Winfrey's vast departure from her childhood upbringing in her grandmother's Baptist church. Oprah precisely remembers her moment of departure from orthodoxy:

> *In my late twenties I remember sitting in church... and this great preacher was preaching about how great God is, how he is omniscient and all-powerful and then he said "God is jealous" and I was caught up in the rapture of that moment until he said "jealous" and something struck me. Something about that didn't feel right in my spirit because I believe that God is love and*

that God is in all things and so that's when the search for something more than doctrine started to stir within me.[2]

Sadly, Oprah's influence is enormous. Millions of people now see her as a spiritual guide and they are departing from the faith with her as they come into agreement with her apostate views. About Oprah's point of departure from the faith my wife wrote:

Oprah talked on the video on my last entry about how the thought of a "jealous" God stopped her pursuit of Him. For me, there is a HUGE amount of security in the jealousy of God... Oprah says, "God is jealous of me?!" And that didn't hit her right. No, God is not jealous OF you; He is jealous FOR you. There's a huge difference in those two little words. Every reference in the Bible to God's jealousy relates to how He feels when the people that He loves forsake Him for other gods. The definition of jealousy supports this: "fearful or wary of being supplanted; apprehensive of losing affection or position." God's LOVE for people makes Him jealous the same way that a devoted spouse would feel if their beloved cheated on him/her.

So, dear Oprah, I find security in the fact that the All Knowing, All Powerful, Magnificent God loves me in such a way that it can be called jealousy. I revel in the security of knowing that I am so loved and protected that not even death kept Him away from me. Knowing the jealousy of God FOR me drives me deeply into His arms rather than flinging me into the place where I have to depend on myself for my salvation.[3]

---

2 Week one of *The New Earth Webclass* offered on oprah.com.
3 Hickey, Kristen. *Jealous God*. midnightcry.wordpress.com. April 4, 2008.

In Zechariah 1:14 God says, *"I am very jealous for Jerusalem and Zion."* The number one thing God has always asked for (wholehearted devotion) will be the number one thing that will sustain us through the trials that are to come. Everything else will burn up.

Our Heavenly Father has a zero-tolerance policy for halfheartedness. Jeremiah 3:14 addresses all of this using the language of spiritual adultery. God said;

> *Return, faithless people, for I am your husband. I will choose you—one from a town and two from a clan and bring you to Zion.*

Verse 10 says, *"in spite of all this, her unfaithful sister Judah did not return to me with all her heart, but only in pretense."*

Religious pretense is a problem today in the Church

When God comes to judge the earth, he won't look at our church buildings—he will look at our hearts. 1 Samuel 16:7 says, *"...the Lord looks at the heart."* 1 Chronicles 28:9 says, *"...the Lord searches every heart..."* What does he specifically look for when he searches our hearts? He looks for wholehearted devotion. This is why David prayed in Psalm 86:11, *"...give me an undivided heart..."* This is why Proverbs 4:23 says, *"... guard your heart."* 1 Corinthians 14:25 says, *"...the secrets of the heart will be laid bare."*

There is much in the Word of God about this. In 1 Kings 8:61 Solomon stood before Israel and shouted with a loud voice, *"...your hearts must be fully committed to the Lord our God..."* Hebrews 12:3, 5 talk about how it is possible to *"lose heart."* Religious pretense and halfheartedness are primary problems in the Church today.

Throughout this book I have been saying the Western church is poised to fall in this end-time apostasy, in part

> ...the Western church is poised to fall in this end-time apostasy, in part because halfheartedness has somehow become the baseline for "normal" believers.

because halfheartedness has somehow become the baseline for "normal" believers. Even in worship, those who get lost in God are often looked upon as strange, when the truth is that wholeheartedness is the most stable foundation.

Immunity from God's end-time judgments

Friends, we are stirring the jealousy of God and the only place of immunity from God's end-time judgments is in consistent wholeheartedness. Consistent means not just for an afternoon. We all have our good moments, but mature believers are those who have nurtured and developed a heart after God. This is what the Lord most wants and what he will most look for in the end-times; those who have turned to him completely. Joel 2:12, 13 says:

> "Now therefore," says the Lord, "Turn to me with all your heart, with fasting, with weeping and with mourning." So rend your heart, and not your garments; return to the Lord your God... [NKJV]

Every time you see those three words—all your heart—it is talking about wholeheartedness. We ought not read over these words too quickly. Sometimes it helps me to slow down and insert the opposite; turn to me with part of your heart.

As I meditate on this, I think of how well I apply it. Am I only turning to him partially? Sometimes I realize the answer is yes, I have God looped in a love triangle. One of the best ways to shut every thing else off is through fasting. That is why this says, turn to me with all your heart, with fasting... We think we can have God and everything else too. This says cut that stuff off. That is how one turns to God with all his heart.

Then it says *rend your hearts, not your garments.* Garments speak of the outward aspects of our lives. God will not look at anything superficial. He looks deep. The word "*rend*" means to tear. The idea is that God asks us to tear our hearts away from everything else. Rending the heart is vivid language that speaks of dealing radically with matters of the heart.

Recently I heard a pro-life leader say that he prayed God would give him a renewed broken heart over abortion. He reached a place where he was speaking all over on the country about abortion and everyday he saw pictures of aborted babies. They eventually became no different to him than any other picture. So he prayed for a renewed broken heart and God gave it to him. Now he cannot look at a picture of an aborted baby without tearing up.

When he told that story, I thought of how frequently I need to pray for God to touch my heart. My point is, we can pray for God to tear our hearts. We can pray, *God, I confess my passion wanes, my oils runs dry, I've lost a sense of your love. I know we only love because you first loved us. God, pour out your love again in a fresh way, such that my heart overflows again. I long for the days when my heart was deeply moved and wholly devoted to you.*

God's three-fold, end-time purpose

God's purpose in the end-times is three-fold; to separate the sincere from the insincere, to remove the hindrances to love, and to purify a people for himself. Daniel 11:35 tells us God's purpose in the end-time tribulation:

...so that they may be refined, purified and made spot-less until the time of the end, for it will still come at the appointed time.

There are many passages in the Bible on this. The fire tests the quality, the fire burns off the impurities, the fire is somehow horrible and good at the same time.

Over the years I have talked to a number of couples who say the tribulation and tragedy they have faced together was both horrible and good. You say, *"Good? How so?"* Good in that it ultimately brought them together in remarkable ways. Sure, they loved each other before but there is something about having things stripped away that brings people back to what is really important.

There are also those who say the opposite. One couple I know never recovered from the death of their daughter. They will tell you the daughter was the only thing they really had in common. Even so, generally, trouble has a way of refining love. Misty Edwards has a song with this line, *"Here it's you and me alone God."*[4] We ought to fight everyday to get to this place where we can say, *it's just you and me here now.* The end-times will take away everything else. I cannot speak for you, but I am increasingly okay with it being *just him here now.* There are times when I say, *"it's just you and me here now."* And God says, *"No your heart is not yet fully here. It's half over there."*

Many are disappointed they do not hear God more often. Consider this, most of the important things I have to say to Kristen I wait to say until we are alone. My sense is God is just waiting for it just to be you and him.

---

4 Brandon Hampton | Misty Edwards | Nina Landis, *Garden,* © 2007 Forerunner Worship

CHAPTER 6

Understanding the Times to Come

One of the books in my library is entitled, "THE BIBLE AND THE NEWSPAPER" by Charles Spurgeon. One hundred-fifty years ago he was making the case that Christians need to keep a Bible in one hand and a newspaper in the other.

People flocked to hear Jesus and, of course, there were several reasons for this, one being that he was always relevant. He spoke God's Word to the times. He helped people understand what they were going through in light of what God wanted to do. He took something timeless and showed its timeliness. I always thought it was amazing how Jesus built a profound teaching off someone's real, immediate felt need.

There are scores of examples in the Gospels. On one occasion someone invited Jesus over for supper and they noticed he didn't wash his hands first. This provided Jesus a platform to say, "*You Pharisees clean the outside of the cup and dish, but inside you are full of greed and wickedness.*" He seized the moment with a message from the Lord.

Here is where I am going with this. We are talking about people in the Church who have no idea about the days in which they live. In this book on apostasy we have considered the reasons people will fall away from the faith in the end-times. To our list of factors fueling the great falling away, we need to add ignorance of the relevance of God's Word.

Is your church clueless?

In the end-times there will be a "clueless camp," even in the Church. The "clueless camp" will not have any real communication with the Lord and they will lack essential information and understanding. As the wrath of God begins to be poured out on the earth, Satan wages war against the people of God, and the great foretold convulsions in nature take place all over the earth, there will be people who have no comprehension of any of this. The only thing they know is what CNN or FOX NEWS feeds them. There will be a disconnect in the minds of many presently sitting in pews between what's in the Bible and what they see unfolding in the world.

1 Thessalonians 5:4 talks about not being in darkness so that this day would overcome you. Those in the dark, not clued in, will be overcome. Why do we study all the chapters in the Bible related to the end-times? Mere curiosity? No. We are students of these passages because Jesus told us to watch and be vigilant. 2 Thessalonians 3:3-11 says that in the end-times, God himself will send a powerful delusion on the earth. If believers aren't solid in their understanding of God's revelation of the days to come, they will fall fast.

In the earlier chapter on STANDING WITH ISRAEL, I quoted Romans 11:25 where Paul says:

> I do not want you to be ignorant of this mystery, brothers...

God's mind regarding the end-times is a mystery to many, but it ought not be. It's not a mystery because God isn't telling us. It's a mystery because it takes wisdom and discernment to receive the revelation. I am not suggesting we can know every detail, but we certainly aren't left in the dark. Most believers today know nothing about the end of the age and frankly, those without understanding will be swept away. There will be "servants" who are surprised and caught off guard at their masters' return. Their lack of understanding will fuel their abandonment of the task.

Here is an apostasy passage from Luke 12:42-46, with my comments and clarifications in parenthesis:

> ...*Who then is the faithful and wise (with understanding) manager, whom the master puts in charge of his servants to give them their food allowance at the proper time? It will be good for that servant whom the master finds doing so when he returns. I tell you the truth; he will put him in charge of all his possessions (it's a promise of our future dominion). But suppose the servant says to himself, "My master is taking a long time in coming," and then he begins to beat the menservants and maidservants (persecute those truly serving Christ for being so fanatical and extreme) and to eat and drink and get drunk (become more like the world). The master of that servant will come on a day when he does not expect him and at an hour he is not aware of. He will cut him to pieces and assign him a place with the unbelievers. (That's a reference to apostasy.)*

In Luke 17:26, Jesus said it will be just like it was in the days of Noah. There will be no sobriety of spirit or awareness of the hour in which they live:

> *People were eating, drinking, marrying and being given in marriage up to the day Noah entered the ark. Then the flood came and destroyed them all.*

You say, *that's not a passage that applies to the Church; that applies to the rest of the world.* Beloved, honestly, six days a week, most of the Church is totally indistinguishable from the world in terms of daily routine and devotion.

Many, even in the Church, do not know what they ought to be doing right now to prepare, they do not know what God is doing now or have any concept of what God is about to do next. They have no grasp of the prophetic timetable or of the sequence that is spelled out in Scripture regarding what will unfold on the earth in the end-times.

Are you apocalyptically agnostic?

Ignorance of the end will be a primary factor in why many in the Church do not finish strong. People will fall away if they don't know what they are hanging on for. One of the things discussed in the OMEGA COURSE is how people often accept one of three extremes about the end-times. The first extreme is being too vague; assuming it's impossible to know what the Scripture says about the end. They are apocalyptically agnostic. Gnosis is the Greek word for knowledge. The agnostic is one with no knowledge. They disengage because they assume all this is not knowable.

> *People will fall away if they don't know what they are hanging on for.*

Another extreme is being too positive; the Church ignoring Scriptures on the extreme pressures of the end. These are the panmillenialists. They just figure it will all pan out in the end. The third extreme is being too negative; pessimillenialism. This is where the Church just draws back and waits for the Rapture. All three groups think it is all about leaving earth and just going to heaven.[1] But us leaving the earth is not at all what is on the

---

1 An important book challenging these popular and traditional but unbiblical notions of the eternal resting place for believers is N.T. Wright's book "*Surprised by Hope: Rethinking Heaven, the Resurrection, and the Mission of the Church*" published by HarperOne in 2008.

mind of Jesus. The Lord Jesus is eager to come back to the earth and set up his Kingdom. He wants us to pray every day that it will be on earth and it is in heaven.

My parents have both died. Did you know the Bible never says they will be floating around on a cloud for eternity? The Bible says the day is drawing nigh when my mother and my father and a host of other saints will be raised from the dead, given resurrected bodies and be back on earth for the Millennial Kingdom and the reign of Christ.

Friends, there is no reason we should be caught unaware as any of this unfolds. This isn't something we are to simply sit back and anticipate. We play a key role praying it into existence. This was one of my favorite parts of the OMEGA COURSE. We studied the seven seals, bowls and trumpets and tried to get more familiar with them. But the part that was new to many was our role in releasing these judgments. The prayer room, dynamically linked to the throne room, will be the governmental center of the earth. As Moses released the judgments on Egypt, in the end-times God will use his praying, prophetic people to pour all this out and drive darkness from the earth (Micah 7:15).

The prayer room, dynamically linked to the throne room, will be the governmental center of the earth.

If we have zero understanding of all this, I believe we will get in the way of God. We ought to know the players in the end-time drama so we are not deceived (including Israel and the company of nations as well as key players like the Two Witnesses, the False Prophet and the Antichrist). In Revelation 17, we read that even John marveled at the Antichrist for a moment. People will marvel at him. He will galvanize the world around himself. The masses will be moved by his speeches. This end-time Antichrist will be quite a convincing figure. Deception will be his number one tool and it is a powerful weapon against the unsuspecting.

The Antichrist will bring a counterfeit peace, solve the terrorism problem, and bring nations together. To the clueless camp in the Christian Church it will seem like an answer to all our prayers. 1 Thessalonians 5:3 says people will be saying, *"peace and safety."* The sobering thing to realize is that many in the *"peace and safety"* crowd will be church people. They will be all for this great ecumenical "let's all come together and hold hands theology" that, in its essence, denies Jesus' leadership in the earth is the only solution.

This time of counterfeit peace will not be an easy time to be a Christian. Many without discernment will defect. Mike Bickle speaks of this time in this way:

> *It will not appear as a time of trouble for those who lack discernment. However, it will be a time of trouble and persecution for the Church...it'll actually be getting worse, but to the untrained eye, it'll look like its getting better...The world will say...What do you Christians want? We finally have peace and you are calling the author of the peace the devil...there is a reason people are leaving your churches in droves.[2]*

Think about this. If John was even wowed by that guy for a moment, how much more will many of our own see him as the earth's solution? Friends, if we are not marveling at Christ and dialed into this mystery, we will be moved by the Antichrist and be swept up in the spirit of the age.

Those lacking spiritual discernment will fall for a counterfeit peace. 1 Thessalonians 5:3 says that while the peace and safety crowd is saying, *"Peace and safety...destruction will come on them suddenly."* Verse 4 then adds, *"But you brothers, are not in*

---

2   Mike Bickle in the *Omega Course.*

darkness so that this day should surprise you…" The word "surprise" is good because to say we will not be surprised is to say we will see it coming. This will be something we are expecting and anticipating. We will be longing for Jesus and rigorously reject those who are crying peace and safety apart from Jesus' leadership in the earth.

The times to come can be known

Understanding is an anointing. I'll explain this in a moment. I Thessalonians 5:2 says, "*For you know very well that the day of the Lord will come like a thief in the night.*" Note the words, "*you know very well...*" Verse one says, "*Now, brothers, about times and dates we do not need to write to you...*" Why?

> *Understanding is an anointing.*

Perhaps because they "*know very well.*" I am not suggesting that we will know precise times and dates, only that we can know (and should know) signs and seasons so we are not caught off guard.

The phrase "*know very well*" is actually a Greek word—akribos. It is the word for precision, or the word "to accurately know." Again, I am not implying we can know the day or the hour, but we will know the generation. We can know the times and seasons. We will know the sequence of events, what to do and what is next.

In 1 Chronicles 12:32 the Bible says the men of Issachar "*… understood the times and knew what Israel should do.*" I believe God has "men of Issachar" in every generation, but particularly in the last generation. We ought to pray for the "Issachar anointing." My prayer is that this whets your appetite for more revelation. Every Saturday morning we have a prayer meeting in our church specifically to cultivate an anointing for the weekend services. We pray that the Issachar anointing would fall on our church and that God would touch previously disengaged and undiscerning people.

The men of Issachar, approximately two hundred in number, knew how to ascertain the periods of the sun and moon, the intercalation of months, the dates of solemn feasts, and they could interpret the signs of the times. Deuteronomy 27:12 says Issachar was positioned on Shechem at Mt. Gerizim "*to bless the people.*" I believe those with the anointing of Issachar understand the timing of God and they possess his heart to release blessing into the earth at the intersection of every season.

These people have a Bible and a newspaper, but they also have a calendar and a compass. How many want that anointing? Who would not want supernatural discernment for the daily news? Many wrongly believe that the Church will be all but abandoned at the end of the age. Nothing could be further from the truth. The Church will not be abandoned; the Church will be anointed at the end of the age.

The Church will not be abandoned; the Church will be anointed at the end of the age.

The prophetic voice will be alive and well. God will speak to people to move here or there, tell them to stay home and they will avert calamity. There will be pockets of mercy, little "Goshens," or shelters, from judgment in the places where there is a praying, prophetic remnant. That's exactly what we are stirring up in our church. We aren't just playing games. We want living encounters with him and we're pressing into vigilance and greater revelation and understanding. Both Jesus and Paul emphasized the knowability of the prophetic signs of the end-times.

In fact, Jesus rebuked Israel for not being able to read the prophetic signs of his coming. Jesus taught that Israel came under judgment for being unresponsive to God because they "*did not know the time of their visitation"* from God. Matthew 16:2-3 says:

> *When evening comes, you say, "It will be fair weather, for the sky is red," and in the morning, "Today it will be stormy, for the sky is red and overcast." You know how to interpret the appearance of the sky, but you cannot interpret the signs of the times.*

The Bible says the prophetic signs will increase in intensity as we get closer to Jesus' return.

Do we live according to God's times and seasons or by the holidays set by HALLMARK CARDS? I'm writing this in 2013. In 2014 and 2015 there will be four eclipses resulting in four blood moons on Jewish feast days. Blood moons on feast days have only happened rarely in the span of several thousand years and each time they have coincided with significant things, which have happened relating to Israel. Luke 21:25 says *"and there will be signs in the sun, and in the moon..."* The sun and moon were created for more than emitting light and marking off days and years. Genesis 1:14 says *"and let them be for signs, and for seasons, and for days and years."* Signs point to something.

> *Do we live according to God's times and seasons or by the holidays set by HALLMARK CARDS?*

The prophetic signs include supernatural signs in the heavens, trends in society, political, military, scientific, technological and economic developments. The prophetic signs serve the Church like a weather station that signals trouble before it comes. They provide a compass in the storm and many will come to Christ in the last days because we have answers—because we rightly interpret the crisis. People who have information change how they live right now.

The prophetic signals and the revelation of Jesus provide the fuel for the prayer movement. If we have no sense for the signs of the times and if our image of Jesus is just the Bible story version we learned about in Sunday school, there will be no zeal in our hearts to pray with fervor for his coming. Jesus told his followers to watch. They fell asleep. How could they fall asleep? Because they were unaware of what was about to unfold.

A greater revelation of Jesus will turn us into worshippers and discerning the signs will turn us into people who pray strategically, in alignment with God's purposes in the earth. Pray specifically for the anointing of Issachar.

CHAPTER 7

The Days of Noah

Those who regularly sit through meetings with me know that I need a whiteboard nearby or at least a clean napkin to draw out what I want to say. Kristen won't let me draw charts when I'm talking to her. But I do when I'm with my kids. If you were to ask my kids which circle they are living in, they would probably say, "*the big circle*" and then they would probably say, "*Obviously my dad sat you down, too.*" The staff at our church all know about the big and little circle. This all started with one of those parenting moments where all the youngsters in my household were freaking out, fussing and fighting about extremely insignificant stuff.

Finally, I had them all sit at the table and I got out pen and paper. First, I drew a great big circle and explained that the circle represents the big issues of life and the world; hunger, poverty, lost and hurting people, the greater purposes of God globally and the Church. All that is big circle stuff. Then I drew a little bitty circle and said that it represents the stuff they are bickering over. My admonition was to stay out of the little circle and they will not bump into one another. Ever since, all I've got to do is mention the big circle and they magically move out of the little circle. Actually, I don't even have to use words. I just fake draw it with my finger and they see it.

Big circle, little circle

Friends, there are a lot of big circle/little circle passages in the Bible. In Matthew 6:33, Jesus said, *"Seek first his kingdom… and all these other things will be added unto you."* In other words, let the big circle stuff that God is doing in the world be your preoccupation and your priority. If you do that, if you stay in that big circle, God will take care of the stuff in your little circle.

It says in Isaiah 55:8 that his ways are not our ways and his thoughts are not our thoughts. God says, *"As the heavens are higher than the earth, so are my ways higher than your ways and my thoughts than your thoughts."*

God is basically inviting us to come up into this great realm—to leave the little circle because there is so much more you. This is the kind of stuff we chew on in staff meetings. We are asking the question, *"So what's the big picture behind what we are doing?"* You ought to stop right in the middle of what you are doing and ask yourself.

A few years ago, I bought a new business book called THE 4-HOUR WORKWEEK,[1] which is not about only working four hours a week. It is about how only about four of the forty hours a week we work are actually hours spent on important and productive stuff. When the author first had this revelation, he made some changes. He realized most of his profits came from a small amount of customers and that 98% of his time was spent chasing the problems that came with the rest of his clientele.

In other words, most of his headaches and unhappiness came from that which produced nothing for him anyway. So he stopped contracting with 95% of his unproductive customers and spent his time on the five productive percent. I share this

---

1 Ferris, Timothy. *The 4-Hour Workweek*. New York: Crown Publishing Group of Random House, 2007.

here to illustrate a very spiritual matter—how most of the world today is caught up in stuff that doesn't produce eternal reward.

The best big circle/little circle passage in the Bible is Matthew 24:37-39. It talks about the end of the age and what it will be like at that time. Jesus said:

> *As it was in the days of Noah, so it will be at the coming of the Son of Man. For in the days before the flood, people were eating and drinking, marrying and giving in marriage, up to the day Noah entered the ark; and they knew nothing about what would happen until the flood came and took them all away. That is how it will be at the coming of the Son of Man.*

This passage says that history will repeat itself except for the part about the world being destroyed by a flood.

The part that will happen again, and the part I would suggest to you *is* happening again, is that, like in the days of Noah, people will be so absorbed in the little affairs of their lives that they have no concept of God's bigger purposes.

There is micro-Christianity and there is macro-Christianity. Micro-Christianity describes the little circle. It is Christian people caught up in how they feel today, what they want, and what will satisfy their needs. Micro-Christianity is about you; your house, your stuff, your pleasure, leisure and treasure (eating/drinking). Macro-Christianity is to engage in the purposes of God. Macro-Christianity is the big circle. It is the big picture of the plans of God.

Micro-Christianity is about you; your house, your stuff, your pleasure, leisure and treasure (eating/drinking). Macro-Christianity is to engage in the purposes of God.

Maybe one of the reasons we are not as productive in terms of advancing the Kingdom of God on earth is because only "four of our forty hours" are spent in the big circle. Maybe our best efforts are being exhausted in the small circle. Maybe we are living again in the days of Noah. Indeed, I believe we are. The following are signs that you are stuck in the small circle. These are signs of the days of Noah.

The only thing you obey is your urges

There is nothing wrong with eating, drinking and marrying, which are the first three things mentioned in verse 38 about the days of Noah. These things are necessary for the preservation of life and the preservation of mankind. But if that is all we are doing, if those urges are the only ones we are obeying, it's as in the days of Noah. One of the things that will jump out at you when you read the story of Noah in Genesis 6 is a phrase that gets repeated. "*Noah did everything just as the Lord had commanded him.*" Noah walked in a remarkable obedience.

This stands out because 1 Peter 3:20 talks about the people in Noah's day living in disobedience. The people who disobeyed long ago when God waited patiently while the ark was being built.

So the days of Noah are marked by people who obey nothing but their own natural urges. It later says in 2 Peter 2 that God "*protected Noah.*" How incredible! God did not spare the ancient world when he brought the flood on its ungodly people, but he protected Noah, a preacher of righteousness, and seven others.

Do you know how God protected Noah? Not the ark. Noah made the ark. Obedience put the protection around Noah. And obeying God, not our urges and inclinations, puts a protection around us from the judgment to come.

Do you know how God protected Noah? Not the ark. Noah made the ark.

106

Obedience put the protection around Noah. And obeying God, not our urges and inclinations, puts a protection around us from the judgment to come.

Absorbed in daily living

The second sign of the days of Noah, or sign you are stuck in the small circle, is you are totally absorbed in daily life. In the same paragraph where Jesus says to seek first the Kingdom and God will take care of the "little circle stuff," Jesus asks, *"Is not life more important than food…"* The answer is *yes*. Yes, there is a greater concern that we ought to occupy ourselves with in this hour.

That is why this is a season of fasting and why I encourage you to start living the fasted lifestyle of the Sermon on the Mount. Through fasting we call on God to supply something beyond bread. We are hungry for his Word and greater understanding. We aren't so absorbed in the day-to-day.

Rejection of the prophetic

The days of Noah will be marked by a rejection of the prophetic. Most people don't realize it took Noah one hundred twenty years to build the ark. God gave ample time for ample prophetic warning, but they were all intentionally tuned out.

Noah, on the other hand, heeded the Word of the Lord no matter how ridiculous it sounded; no matter how many scoffers were out there saying there isn't a cloud in the sky. 2 Peter 3:3-7 says it will be the same at the end of the age:

First of all, you must understand that in the last days scoffers will come, scoffing and following their own evil desires. They will say, "Where is this 'coming' he promised? Ever since our fathers died, everything goes on as it has since the beginning of creation." But they deliberately forget that long ago by God's word the heavens existed and the earth was formed out of water and by water. By these waters also the world of that time was deluged and destroyed. By the same word the present heavens and earth are reserved for fire, being kept for the day of judgment and destruction of ungodly men.

This passage says God's Word is the instigator of all that happens, all that has been and all that will be.

An acceptance of, an ear for, and an understanding of the prophetic word will mean salvation in the days ahead. The phrase *"deliberately forget"* means they intentionally rejected the prophetic word. Literally rendered it could read, *they wished it were not so.* (Like "wishing" could actually change anything.) The popular paraphrase THE MESSAGE says they, *"conveniently forgot"* to notice. This leads me to the fourth mark of the days of Noah; that, despite ample warnings, you've yet to prepare.

> *An acceptance of, an ear for, and an understanding of the prophetic word will mean salvation in the days ahead.*

Despite ample warnings, you've yet to prepare

Preparation is something we do in faith. Hebrews 11:8 says, *"By faith Noah, when warned about things not yet seen, in holy fear, built an ark to save his family."*

The story of Noah is not just about being a hearer of the word; it's about being a doer of the word. He would have perished like all the rest had he heard the word and spent his one hundred twenty years doing what all the others did. One of the things that Mike Bickle frequently says is that he's, *"thankful for the Lord's patience 'cause right now* [he does] *not think IHOP is fully prepared for either the triumph or the trauma yet to come."*

Wow. If the INTERNATIONAL HOUSE OF PRAYER is not yet prepared, who is?

And that's why I frequently teach and write about the Sermon on the Mount. It's the workout program for the fasted lifestyle. It's the best place in the Bible to prepare yourself for what's coming. People who run marathons prepare themselves. The Bible, in numerous places, speaks of how many will fall away and not cross the finish line because they had no stamina for suffering and no understanding for why God would allow things to unfold as they do.

If your church exists just to give you a weekly fix, you're missing it. A weekly fix will fix nothing. We are here to raise up a generation whose lives are lived in the big circle, not wasted in the little circle. He wants to launch people into the big circle.

There is an absence of the fear of the Lord

The fifth mark of the days of Noah is how there will be an absence of the fear of the Lord. People will not only be preoccupied, they will be unconcerned. Hebrews 11:7 says, "*...when warned about things not yet seen, in holy fear built an ark.*"

The Matthew 24 text says people will be "*eating and drinking, marrying...up to the day Noah entered the ark.*" In other words, life for them will be normal. It will go on as always and that time will come with a shattering suddenness on those who are stuck in the small circle. However, those in the big circle walk in a reverence, or a holy fear, of the bigger moments that are taking place. People who are unafraid are simply people who are unaware, which is number six on the list. There is a widespread ignorance of the unfolding plans of God.

A widespread ignorance of the unfolding plans of God

The days of Noah are days where people are preoccupied, unconcerned and unaware. Matthew 24:39 says, "...*they knew nothing about what would happen...*" They are stuck down in the little circle. They can tell you the cast members of their favorite television shows, but couldn't name the prophets or what they had to say about the hour in which we live.

One of the reasons people who are presently standing with Christ will deliberately walk away from him under the pressure of the end-times is that they have no understanding for why God would allow what he will allow to happen on earth. People will get mad at God because they have no clue what he's up to in terms of his plans for the nations or his purposes for humankind.

Anger is increasing and a proclivity toward violence is evident

Number seven on my list of marks of the days of Noah is that anger is increasing in society and individuals and a proclivity toward violence is evident.

Genesis 6 says that in the days of Noah the earth was corrupt and filled with violence; not pure, not peaceable. People in the small circle fight. Church people in the small circle fight and are critical—they strain gnats and swallow camels.[2] They are negative, critical, and nasty to each other. During this time, society at large will assume the disposition of the Beast whose nature is cruel. I used the phrase proclivity toward violence because these will be days when people turn on each other. Earlier in Matthew 24, Jesus talked about nation against nation, but he also said the love of most will grow cold and this will be a time when brothers betray brothers, relatives and friends.

---

2   Matthew 23:24

Just in the last few weeks there have been reports that a father killed his two children and a grandson killed his grandmother. Many nations are gripped in violence unimaginable. However it's escalating here in America too. We teach kids they are just the next random mutation in an unguided evolutionary process and then we wonder why they have little regard for others and no concept of the sanctity of human life. We teach kids the fixed rule of "life" is *survival of the fittest* and then wonder why bullying and school shootings are increasing. A steady diet of violent video games and movies is feeding something in society we don't want to feed.

We rarely watch television anymore but we were channel surfing the night and five channels in a row illustrated our proclivity toward violence. People tune in to see cops beating people, high speed chases gone bad and cheaters getting beat up by spouses who catch them in adultery. Cage fighting is now a three billion dollar industry, the fastest growing sport in the world. Bloodlusting, rubbernecking, pay-per-view crowds cheer on cage fighters elbowing each other in the face as if it were a legitimate "sport." Promoters sell *"King of the Cage: Greatest Knockouts #19."* What's next, bringing back the gladiators? Society is losing it's capacity to wince. Why is all this so popular? Here's why–these are the days of Noah where there is a marked proclivity toward violence.

> *Society is losing it's capacity to wince.*

Relationships will not last

It dawned on me that this line about *"marrying and giving up in marriage"* could refer to the divorce rate today. My friend told me that between her and her husband's four biological parents there have been twelve divorces! The days of Noah will be marked by people turning on each other. The list could be much longer—I've tried to only put down the major signs. In light of

111

this giving up in marriage verse and the parable of the ten virgins in Matthew 25, it dawned on me to add an eighth mark of the days of Noah to the list.

Seeking the wrong bridegroom

The end-times are about the Bride, the Church, being united with the Bridegroom Jesus. Jesus said many will come to him in that day and he will say, *away from me I never knew you.*[3] There will be two groups—those who have sought intimacy with Him and those who sought intimacy elsewhere. People in the little circle don't have a consistent prayer life. They surely throw up a few prayers for their stuff, but they do not seek him. They have not sought him. They have not pursued him.

The days of Noah will be days of misplaced intimacy, where people love the wrong thing, loving pleasure, not of God. Here I will share a short list stating the opposite of all that we have just walked through. These are eight indicators you are in the big circle of God's global redemptive purposes.

> *The days of Noah will be days of misplaced intimacy, where people love the wrong thing...*

1. You fast and pray more than you eat and drink. You long for his coming!

2. His return is more on your mind than your recreation (or retirement).

3. You are hungry for the prophetic word and see the Bible's extreme relevance.

4. Your friends are also preparing for the Day of the Lord.

---

3   Matthew 7:21-23

5. Obeying God meticulously, in holy fear, is your preoccupation.

6. Love for people and urgency are in your spirit.

7. You are leaving the small circle stuff in God's hands.

8. You read the newspaper (at least in an electronic format)!

That last one is the modern day equivalent of looking for rain clouds.

This goes beyond merely subscribing to your local daily newspaper. I'm talking about being a Christian who has a grasp and understanding of what is transpiring in the world. Modern day geo-politics is the arena in which the big circle events of the Bible are played out. The prophetic passages of long ago are unfolding today and few in the world recognize what is and what is yet to come because they are stuck in the little circle.

CHAPTER 8

The Skyrocketing Cost of Discipleship

Jesus paid the highest and ultimate price for us yet so many think following him is free. The day is not far off when those of us who have given our lives to Christ might actually have to give our lives for Christ.

When we come to Jesus, he asks for our everything. Of course, our everything up to that point doesn't amount to much. We're trading our mess for his perfection. Very few people look back

> *The day is not far off when those of us who have given our lives to Christ might actually have to give our lives for Christ.*

at their moment of salvation and wonder if it was worth it. However, as we grow in our walk with God, we become more and more aware of what he is asking of us. He's not just interested in changing our behavior; he also wants to change our thoughts. He's not simply addressing our actions; he reaches deep into our motives. Five, ten or twenty years down the road we are continuing to surrender ever more delicate parts of our lives as we align ourselves more with what he is calling us to.

In seeking to become disciples of Christ, we discover that the cost grows over time as we grow closer to him, and we are subsequently more willing to pay the price. There is another factor that contributes to what I call the skyrocketing cost of discipleship and this factor will weigh on each of us in coming years. Just as Jesus asks more of us over time, the times will demand more of us as well. Not all days are created equal, and days to come are actually designed to stretch each of us in our pursuit of God.

The price is only going up

There is a cost to discipleship, a high cost. And the price is only going up, way way up as we proceed toward the end of the age. Maybe this chapter should have been first instead of last because one of the main reasons people will fall away at the end of the age is because the price to follow Christ will get too high. In fact, the cost of following Christ will skyrocket. In Luke 14:25-27 Jesus forewarned that following him will cost people even the relationships they presently hold dearest; father, mother, wife and children. He said we each need to calculate this high cost.

> *Suppose one of you wants to build a tower. Will he not first sit down and estimate the cost to see if he has enough money to complete it. For if he lays the foundation and is not able to finish it...*

Jesus was speaking parabolically about people who start following him and fall away. Jesus then referenced a king about to go to war against another king asking, will he not first sit down and calculate if he has the strength to fight to the finish? His point is that the Christian life isn't easy, in fact it's a battle and the day is coming when the battle will rage with unprecedented intensity against Christ and his Church.

In Matthew 24, Jesus warns that the falling away at the end of the age will be in part because people are not willing to die for Him in martyrdom:

"Then you will be handed over to be persecuted and put to death, and you will be hated by all nations because of me. At that time, many will turn away from the faith..."

As Bonhoeffer famously wrote; *"the call to Christ is a call to come and die."*

Today people have a fraidy cat view of death seeing it as the worst thing that could happen-- as the end, as a travesty, as a total loss, as the worst that could happen. God sees it very differently. To him death leads to life; *unless a grain of wheat falls to the ground and dies it remains only a seed* (John 12:24). Confidence in facing death comes from good theology. Ungodly beliefs about death and dying will result in people deciding not to pay this high price to follow the path of Christ to our own cross.

The Gospel that is preached in so many places is about life and resurrection but few are reminded and readied for the reality that crucifixion comes before resurrection. People aren't hearing that message and some even teach Jesus suffered so we don't have to or that we will escape tribulation, both of which are clear deviations from 1 Timothy 3:12... *"In fact, everyone who wants to live a godly life in Christ Jesus will be persecuted."*

> *Confidence in facing death comes from good theology. Ungodly beliefs about death and dying will result in people deciding not to pay this high price to follow the path of Christ to our own cross.*

Self-preservation is not a Christian virtue. It is certainly a human instinct but it is not a Christian virtue. A Christian virtue is... *"greater love has no one than this, that he lay his life down for others"* (John 15:13). Also, a fear of death is not a Christian concern. In the Sermon on the Mount Jesus said, *"Give no thought to your life... Who of you by worrying can add a single hour to his life?"* (Matthew 6:25, 27) He was teaching us to not worry about preserving or prolonging our lives.

The grace of martyrdom

There is a grace or spiritual provision for suffering and persecution; in fact, martyrdom is a spiritual gift. How could it be a gift? Certainly it would be the gift that no one wants! My friend and teacher Dr. C. Peter Wagner wrote the classic book on spiritual gifts and he always gets a chuckle when he says martyrdom is the one spiritual gift you aren't sure you have until you need it and it's the only spiritual gift you can only use once! Levity aside, spiritual gifts aren't toys to play with, they are graces for spiritual breakthrough. There is a grace to give up your life for Christ.

Martyrs are sustained by grace and propelled by love. The propellant behind the grace of martyrdom is love. But for many believers the end of the age will be a time when their love grows cold. Martyrdom is simultaneously a holy detachment and a holy attachment, as we love Jesus not so much our lives. Revelation 12:11 says *"...they did not love their lives so much as to shrink from death."* Some people bristle when I connect the dots between money and end-day American materialism with our unwillingness to give our lives. Letting go comes natural for the martyr as they have lived a life of faithful giving in the little things. If you can't give your stuff, you won't give your life. If you can't give your money, what makes you think you'd be willing to pay the skyrocketing cost of discipleship?

> **The propellant behind the grace of martyrdom is love. But for many believers the end of the age will be a time when their love grows cold.**

In the Beatitudes Jesus said this is the path God blesses and the one we should expect; *"Blessed are those who are persecuted... for in the same way they persecuted the prophets who were before you"* (Matthew 5:10, 12). In other words, it won't be any different for you than it was for them. Hebrews tells us they were flogged, put in chains, imprisoned, stoned, sawed in two and went about destitute, persecuted and mistreated (Hebrews 11:36-37).

At the culmination of the age when evil retaliates against everything that is good, followers of Christ will face these refining fires. During that time of Great Tribulation, to use the familiar expression: many will get out of the kitchen because they can't take the heat. That's what this chapter is about - apostasy will be seen as an escape from martyrdom.

The world is increasingly a dangerous place for Christians. Globally, in unprecedented numbers, Christians are being beaten, imprisoned and killed. Yet here in America, pastors preach "dying to ourselves" to people sitting in comfortable chairs and then they serve jelly donuts and STARBUCKS after the service. The normal Christian life for most westerners is two or three Sunday mornings a month in church with a vague idea that we should be applying what we have learned there during the week. In our culture, faith is measured in such subtle ways that we have neighbors who we think *"might be Christians... but we're not sure,"* and they may have the same thoughts about us.

> *Yet here in America, pastors preach "dying to ourselves" to people sitting in comfortable chairs and then they serve jelly donuts and STARBUCKS after the service.*

Watchman Nee was a leader in the Chinese church for decades. Christianity Today lists him as one of the 100 most influential Christians of the last century. His book THE NORMAL CHRISTIAN LIFE, is full of bold statements like this one: *"What the Lord Jesus looks for in us is a life laid at his feet."* In Watchman Nee's setting, the normal Christian life was much different. He was fiercely persecuted after the Communists took over China in 1949. After being thrown in prison on a ridiculous array of false charges, he was held there for the last 20 years of his life. Watchman Nee's 'normal' was very different than ours. The question to ask is *"Whose version of normal should be expected?"*

If you look at church history, our insulated view of normal is a relatively new and untried one. For most of its existence – certainly during its time of greatest growth – the Church encountered outright resistance from the culture, the authorities and Satan. In fact, for those brief seasons where the Church was untested, we find that she quickly grew lackadaisical, inward and sinful. There is a wrong idea circulating in certain Christian circles that says the days of persecution are over. That idea could only circulate inside the closed loop of Americanized, cultural Christianity because if you expand very far in time or geography, it would be hard to find people who agreed with that.

Historically, we have referred to the first two centuries as the age of persecution or martyrdom. All of Jesus' disciples except for John were martyred. For generations to come, it was the expectation of the church. Jesus words in Matthew 16:24 echoed in their ears. *"If anyone would come after me, he must deny himself and take up his cross and follow me."* Christians in those days would have well remembered His cross and the price it exacted from His body.

Church historian Stephen Neill wrote *"Every Christian in the first century knew that sooner or later he might have to testify to his faith at the cost of his life."* We look back at the days of the Romans throwing Christians to the lions and mop our brow with relief that we were blessed to be born so much after the fact, believing that the age of martyrs is over and somehow we escaped. Again, our narrow point of view deludes us.

The three colors of martyrdom

For numerous reasons (aside from my Irish heritage), I track with the Celtic daily prayer rhythm and traditions. In Thomas Cahill's best selling book HOW THE IRISH SAVED CIVILIZATION, he talks about how God used fourth and fifth century Irish monks to copy and hide away literature, history, art and the riches of ancient philosophy and science preserving a vast treasury of knowledge through the period of the Dark Ages.

My contention is that throughout Church history, God raised up vibrant and faithful prayer movements (monasticism) when Christianity came into periods of compromise and crisis. A Celtic monk in the seventh century named Cambrai, in what we call THE CAMBRAI HOMILY, outlined three categories of martyrdom designated by colors; red, green and white. (The term *white martyrdom* was first used by St. Jerome, a desert hermit in the third century).

Red martyrdom refers to when blood is shed; when they lop off your head or throw you to the lions. If Christ is indeed first, our safety and security are at least a distant second. You may see safety-first signs around your place of employment, but safety-first is not a Christian priority. Christ and his Kingdom come first.

...safety-first is not a Christian priority.

In Matthew 10:38 Jesus said *"anyone who does not take his cross and follow me is not worthy of me."* Long before the crucifixion of Jesus, he made the cross the symbol of Christian discipleship. What does discipleship look like? Is the symbol of discipleship an easy chair? Is it a remote control where we push buttons so God changes things for us? Is it a pair of hiking books? Is the symbol of discipleship a white surrender flag? Close, but not quite. The symbol of discipleship looks like a cross. And Jesus is not saying here to *drag your cross with great reluctance and resentment toward it.* He's saying *take it up and embrace it.*

Interestingly, the Celtic saints never faced a period of red martyrdom but they still knew the call of Christ was to lose your life to find it. So Cambrai spoke also of *green martyrdom* to refer to those who leave behind comforts and pleasures, deny their flesh, assuming vows of poverty and chastity or living simply and frugally. You can easily see this in the priesthood in America and globally, and certainly in the various forms of old and new monasticism all alive and well in Christendom today. Even in evangelicalism there are people who live simply (having *wartime mentalities* and living *wartime lifestyles*[1]) so they can be a greater blessing. That's green martyrdom, selling your possessions to follow Christ. It's the ascetic life; practicing rigorous self-discipline and abstinence from all forms of indulgence. If Christ is first, comfort and convenience can't be.

The daily cross is the antithesis of comfort. Yet for some today coming to Christ means find a comfortable seat on Sunday. It means it needs to fit into my schedule. It means the inconvenience factor needs to be real low. It means Jesus better not be too demanding. Comfort-first means my well-being is the first consideration and the Kingdom of God is second.

> *The daily cross is the antithesis of comfort. Yet for some today coming to Christ means find a comfortable seat on Sunday.*

White martyrdom is the separation from loved ones. At one level it's kissing your family goodbye before getting on a ship to sail to a faraway place to spend your life reaching the people God calls you to reach. Perhaps you are thinking how glad you

---

1   The late Ralph Winter, a missiologist at the US Center for World Mission in Pasadena California used the term "wartime lifestyles" to teach austerity and simplicity encouraging Christians to live only on what we need and give the rest of our income where it is needed most.

are that God hasn't put a call like that on your life. In my case I'm thankful my family can do missions right alongside me. It's what we do together.

Please consider what white martyrdom means for you. Honestly, some families are so about their "family" and family activities that the Kingdom of God and the priorities of the Kingdom of God are on the back burner. If Christ is first, even your family can't be. In Luke 14:26 Jesus even said:

If anyone comes to me and does not hate his father and mother, his wife and children, his brothers and sisters– yes, even his own life– he cannot be my disciple.

This doesn't mean we neglect our families. It's about making him so obviously first in our lives that our most cherished things and even our most cherish family members take a distant second. In Mark 10:28 Peter said to Jesus, *"we have left everything to follow you."* To that Jesus replied in verses 29-30:

I tell you the truth, no one who has left home or brothers or sisters or mother or father or children or fields for me and the gospel will fail to receive a hundred times as much in this present age (homes, brothers, sisters, mothers, children and fields – and with them persecutions) and in the age to come, eternal life.

Martyrdom comes in a variety of forms and is a normal part of taking up our daily cross. It is the path, the narrow difficult road of discipleship, that leads to life.

The latter age of martyrdom

Of the 45,400,000 people who have been martyred for faith in Jesus, 65% of those have been killed within the last hundred years. Worldwide, martyrdom is more common than ever. While this may be shocking to us, it shouldn't be. We have managed to reduce Jesus' words about taking up our cross to mean anything but laying down our lives, but how can we misinterpret his remarks in Matthew 24:9-14?

> *Then you will be handed over to be persecuted and put to death, and you will be hated by all nations because of me. At that time, many will turn away from the faith and will betray and hate each other, and many false prophets will appear and deceive many people. Because of the increase of wickedness, the love of most will grow cold, but he who stands firm to the end will be saved. And this gospel of the kingdom will be preached in the whole world as a testimony to all nations, and then the end will come.*

In these few sentences, Jesus draws the road map for what will come to his followers as history plays itself out. He vividly describes martyrdom, international pursuit, betrayal, an increase in evil and a church victorious in preaching the kingdom of God to the ends of the earth. Granted, there are some theologians who insist this passage happened in 70AD when Jerusalem fell to the Romans, but that conquest had nothing to do with Christianity. It was a military campaign against Israel. In fact, most of the Christian population had been exiled by that time. If Jesus was warning his followers about 70AD, either he misunderstood the threat or got the details of their future wrong. It would be convenient and comfortable to believe this passage has already been fulfilled, but it wouldn't be Biblical.

If this passage points to our future, then many of us are staring at a very different course of life than we have been conditioned to anticipate. Take a moment to investigate the chart on the next page, where 1815 marks the beginning of what I call the Early Modern Period. It is notable that roughly at this point in history, there was a divergence between the persecuted church and the comfortable church.

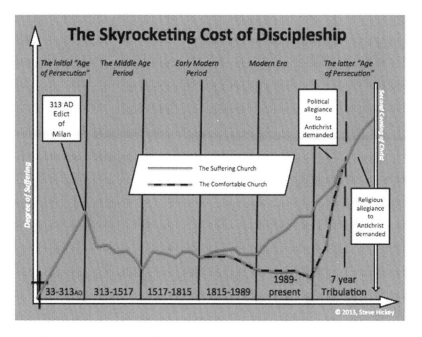

Since that marker in time, two churches have spread across the globe with slightly differing theologies and massively different experiences.

Two churches a world apart

While both teach of a Jesus that saves from eternal hell, the comfortable church forms its ideas of the expected normal Christian life based on its experience, which does not include persecution. In the comfortable church, life is relatively easy. Their faith is expressed without challenge, and lacking that resistance, their faith is often weak. The persecuted church, however, has developed a very different perspective of suffering. They see it as a normal part of one's faith. To choose faith in this setting is to acknowledge the persecution that will undoubtedly accompany it.

The expected ease of the comfortable church and the anticipated struggle of the persecuted church causes a distinct and increasing difference in their experience and expression of faith. The comfortable church, over time, grows comfortable not only with their faith but with the world around them. There is little sense of warfare, of darkness, or even a difference between them and the unchurched masses that surround them. The comfortable church gives us ecumenicalism and the CO-EXIST movement (see page 36) because they see little difference in their own faith and the faith of others.

The persecuted church, however, grows more uncomfortable as a result of their stand for Christ. They fully understand that they are living in a dark world and are driven to be a source of light. They are faced daily with the differences between their faith and the false idol worship that surrounds and persecutes them. They understand that their faith and those false religions cannot and do not coexist.

While most of the comfortable church knows that the persecuted church exists and even supports it through groups like VOICE OF THE MARTYRS, they also hold an attitude best described as *"there but for the grace of God go I...."* In other words, *"Wow. How terrible. God has been so good to me. I'm glad that won't ever happen."* I wonder how that sounds to the persecuted church? I wonder if they know their comfortable cousins are on the other side of the globe selfishly appreciating that they are somehow different.

America needs an Amos to prophetically challenge our delusions that all this wealth and comfortable living can't be taken away, that our nation has reached an untouchable status believing the things that happen elsewhere won't ever happen to us. They can, overnight, and at some point they will.

The comfortable church and the persecuted church will not be different forever. As time marches on and the Tribulation begins, the comfortable church will quickly sense a shift in the wind. At first it will be a shift in society. Their values, though not dramatically different than those of the unchurched, will stand out in the crowd because of their attachment to Jesus. In the beginning of the Tribulation, benevolence and meeting the needs of others for humanitarian reasons will be in vogue. Doing it in the name of Jesus will draw stares and the first wave of resistance that the comfortable church is likely to perceive.

• • • • • • • • • • • • • • • • • •

The comfortable church and the persecuted church will not be different forever. As time marches on and the Tribulation begins, the comfortable church will quickly sense a shift in the wind.

• • • • • • • • • • • • • • • • • •

One example of this beginning is found in the experience of my friend Benjamin Nolot, the founder of EXODUS CRY and the producer of a film called NEFARIOUS: THE MERCHANT OF SOULS. The documentary exposes the breadth and depth of the sex trafficking industry and clearly illustrates the role of Jesus in bringing justice to the earth. NEFARIOUS has attracted a lot of attention and 24 major film festival awards to date.

Recently, Nolot was approached by a group of top tier Hollywood operatives who wanted to arrange a screening for their A-list peers in Hollywood. Nolot knew this would raise awareness for the film and potentially raise a lot of much needed money for the movie's sequel. They only had one request – that he edit out the clear references to Jesus at the end of the film. Because he is a man of character, Nolot politely refused.

Jesus will be pushed out of our culture in increasingly forceful ways as the Tribulation begins. People will desire spirituality but rebuff the idea of a redeemer. Members of the comfortable church will be split. Some will go the way of culture. Others will grow deeper in their faith. Those that grow deep will realize that they are becoming more and more like their persecuted cousins. Over time, the persecuted and comfortable church will become one. It will be far more painful for the comfortable church than it will be for the persecuted church, because the comfortable church will endure the greater rate of change. They will be comfortable no longer.

Most of us grew up with at least a limited sense of entitlement – if not to a certain standard of living, at least to a certain measure of safety. We grew up watching hostility around the world on the evening news but it was a fairly academic exercise. We knew that it was happening somewhere, but those things didn't happen in America. We were different. We were insulated. Safety within our borders was almost considered an inalienable right. What if our brief mental snapshot of history is wrong and the Bible is right? If the cost of following Jesus escalates to the level that he tells us it will? Will a comfortable church that has resisted pain at all cost suddenly be prepared to pay that price?

Martyrs are a unique breed even though history, prophecy and common sense tell us that they shouldn't be. From its inception, the Church has been the target of rage from the enemy and his minions. Scripture tells us that rage will not abate as the clock of natural history ticks towards zero. Revelation 12:12 tells us that Satan will roam the earth filled with rage at that time. Simple logic tells us that having aligned with one side – even the victorious side – will make us a target for the other side. If Satan is truly to roam the earth filled with rage, who do we presume to be his target? Many confess Jesus and claim to do so *"for better or worse."* However, then they seem shocked that 'worse' may include surrendering their earthly life even though they would have said they surrendered everything at the cross when they began the journey.

• • • • • • • • • • • • • • • • • •

Many confess Jesus and claim to do so "for better or worse." However, then they seem shocked that 'worse' may include surrendering their earthly life...

• • • • • • • • • • • • • • • • • •

A life laid down isn't a life wasted

The idea of martyrdom makes us uneasy. It's not just the avoidance of pain that motivates us, although that is very real for all of us. No one likes the idea of physical suffering. More than that though, it's the perception that a martyr accomplishes nothing. We think that if we die in defense of truth, no one will be left to fight the fight. What does the body of a martyr accomplish? Does it convince any of its oppressors that it somehow won the debate? Or does it just lay there on the floor until it is carried away by other believers also destined for death?

Joseph Ton was a Romanian pastor who published a sermon calling for churches to resist the Communist government's control over their ministries. When he was confronted by the secret police, they insisted that he renounce his own sermons.

"No, sir!" Ton retorted. *"I will not do that!"*

Shock reverberated through the police station. Romanians did not routinely resist an order from the secret police. The Romanians were a proud people but resisting this powerful force never ended well. The police sergeant in charge of interrogation pressed harder.

"Aren't you aware that I am authorized to use force against you?" he asked. For the secret police, force was not a legal term. It meant beatings, torture and sometimes murder.

Pastor Ton swallowed hard and answered. *"Sir, let me explain that to you. You see, your supreme weapon is killing. My supreme weapon is dying. You know that my sermons are spread all over the country on tapes. When you kill me, I only sprinkle them with my blood. They will speak ten times louder after that because everyone will say 'That preacher meant it because it was sealed with his blood!'. So go on, sir, kill me. When you kill me, I will win the supreme victory."*

The secret police released him, knowing his martyrdom would be far more of a problem than his sermons.

You may read this and think *"That doesn't apply to me. I have no sermons to sprinkle with my blood. If I were to die right now, even for my faith, what would it mean?"* In reality, you have been preaching sermons with your life. What has your life meant so far? Whatever you have stood for will mean volumes more when punctuated by your martyrdom.

If you have stood for nothing until this point, your death really would be for naught. If you have stood for Christ and are known for your faith, then even in your martyrdom you are preaching. In fact, you are preaching the loudest message of your life. Because of this, the martyrs of the persecuted church will be the most effective of the end-time evangelists as they have lived their lives proclaiming truths that the comfortable church believed but kept to themselves.

There is a second and even greater reason that martyrdom matters. No martyr truly dies in vain. Revelation 6:10-11 tells us that in the end, Jesus will avenge their blood.

> *'How long, Sovereign Lord, holy and true, until you judge the inhabitants of the earth and avenge our blood?' Then each of them was given a white robe, and they were told to wait a little longer, until the number of their fellow servants and brothers who were to be killed as they had been was completed.*

Those who pay the ultimate cost of discipleship, who do not love their lives unto death, will serve to punctuate the greatest sentence of all time. It is one that says that God is just and will not forget those who call upon Him.

All this talk of suffering and difficulty goes against our natural sense of order and peace. Primarily that is because we see it disconnected from purpose. The comfortable church calls all suffering 'senseless.' The persecuted church calls suffering 'training.' On the day when they are proven right, we will all proclaim, *"Great and marvelous are Your works, Lord God Almighty. Just and true are Your ways."*

In the end, that will be the mark of a true disciple of Jesus.

Other books by Steve Hickey

- *Obtainable Expectations: Timely Exposition Jesus' Sermon on the Mount*

    (BRIDGE-LOGOS, 2012)

- *Obtainable Destiny: Timely Exposition of the Apostolic Letters - 1, 2 Timothy & Titus*

    (CREATION HOUSE, 2004)

- *Momentum: God's Ever Increasing Kingdom*

    (CREATION HOUSE, 2009)

- *The Fall Away Factor*

    (ONE SENT BOOKS, 2013)

Steve's books are available on Amazon.com
or email him directly: steve@churchatthegate.com

29267639R00077

Made in the USA
Lexington, KY
19 January 2014